CAMBRIDGE LIBRARY COLLECTION

Books of enduring scholarly value

History

The books reissued in this series include accounts of historical events and movements by eye-witnesses and contemporaries, as well as landmark studies that assembled significant source materials or developed new historiographical methods. The series includes work in social, political and military history on a wide range of periods and regions, giving modern scholars ready access to influential publications of the past.

Pamphlets on West Indian Slavery

This book contains two pamphlets showing two diametrically opposed points of view on the slavery question. British philanthropist Elizabeth Heyrick (1769–1831) was a strong supporter of complete emancipation for African slaves in the British West Indies, and published *Immediate, Not Gradual Abolition* in 1824. This work not only criticises anti-slavery campaigners of the time, such as William Wilberforce and Thomas Clarkson, whose efforts Heyrick considered too cautious and indirect; they also call for a boycott of all slave-produced goods from the West Indies – particularly sugar – and underline the collective responsibility of British citizens in the matter. Alexander McDonnell (1794–1875) was an equally vigorous propagandist for the sugar-planters of the West Indies, and published *Compulsory Manumission: or, An Examination of the Actual State of the West India Question*, in 1827. These two works show the strength of feeling on both sides of the argument in Britain nearly twenty years after the abolition of the slave trade itself.

Cambridge University Press has long been a pioneer in the reissuing of out-of-print titles from its own backlist, producing digital reprints of books that are still sought after by scholars and students but could not be reprinted economically using traditional technology. The Cambridge Library Collection extends this activity to a wider range of books which are still of importance to researchers and professionals, either for the source material they contain, or as landmarks in the history of their academic discipline.

Drawing from the world-renowned collections in the Cambridge University Library, and guided by the advice of experts in each subject area, Cambridge University Press is using state-of-the-art scanning machines in its own Printing House to capture the content of each book selected for inclusion. The files are processed to give a consistently clear, crisp image, and the books finished to the high quality standard for which the Press is recognised around the world. The latest print-on-demand technology ensures that the books will remain available indefinitely, and that orders for single or multiple copies can quickly be supplied.

The Cambridge Library Collection will bring back to life books of enduring scholarly value (including out-of-copyright works originally issued by other publishers) across a wide range of disciplines in the humanities and social sciences and in science and technology.

Pamphlets on
West Indian Slavery

Elizabeth Heyrick
Alexander McDonnell

CAMBRIDGE
UNIVERSITY PRESS

CAMBRIDGE UNIVERSITY PRESS

Cambridge, New York, Melbourne, Madrid, Cape Town, Singapore,
São Paolo, Delhi, Dubai, Tokyo, Mexico City

Published in the United States of America by Cambridge University Press, New York

www.cambridge.org
Information on this title: www.cambridge.org/9781108020305

This edition first published 1824-7
This digitally printed version 2010

ISBN 978-1-108-02030-5 Paperback

IMMEDIATE,

NOT

GRADUAL ABOLITION;

OR,

AN INQUIRY

INTO THE SHORTEST, SAFEST, AND MOST EFFECTUAL
MEANS OF GETTING RID OF

WEST INDIAN SLAVERY.

LONDON:

SOLD BY J. HATCHARD AND SON, 187, PICCADILLY;

AND BY THOMAS COMBE, LEICESTER.

MDCCCXXIV.

IMMEDIATE,

NOT

GRADUAL ABOLITION,

&c. &c. &c.

IT is now seventeen years since the *Slave Trade* was abolished by the Government of this country—but *Slavery* is still perpetuated in our West India colonies, and the horrors of the Slave Trade are aggravated rather than mitigated. By making it felony for British subjects to be concerned in that inhuman traffic, England has only transferred her share of it to other countries. She has, indeed, by negociation and remonstrance, endeavoured to persuade them to follow her example. —But has she succeeded?—How should she, whilst there is so little consistency in her conduct? Who will listen to her pathetic declamations on the injustice and cruelty of the Slave Trade— whilst she rivets the chains upon her own slaves,

A

and subjects them to all the injustice and cruelty which she so eloquently deplores when her own interest is no longer at stake? Before we can have any rational hope of prevailing on our guilty neighbours to abandon this atrocious commerce, —to relinquish the gain of oppression,—the wealth obtained by rapine and violence,—by the deep groans, the bitter anguish of our unoffending fellow creatures ;—we must purge ourselves from these pollutions ;—we must break the iron yoke from off the neck of *our own slaves,*—and let the wretched captives in our own islands go free. Then, and not till then, we shall speak to the surrounding nations with the *all-commanding eloquence of sincerity and truth,*—and our persuasions will be backed by the *irresistible argument of consistent example.* But to invite others to be just and merciful whilst we grasp in our own hands the rod of oppression,—to solicit others to relinquish the wages of iniquity whilst we are putting them into our own pockets—what is it but cant and hypocrisy? Do such preachers of justice and mercy ever make converts ? On the contrary,—do they not render themselves ridiculous and contemptible?

But let us, *individually,* bring this great question closely home to our own bosoms. We that hear, and read, and approve, and applaud the powerful appeals, the irrefragable arguments against the Slave Trade, and against slavery,—are we *ourselves* sincere, or hypocritical? Are *we* the true friends of justice, or do we only cant about it?—To which party do *we* really belong? —to the friends of emancipation, or of perpetual slavery? Every individual belongs to one party or the other; not speculatively, or professionally merely, but practically. The perpetuation of slavery in our West India colonies, is not an abstract question, to be settled between the Government and the Planters,—it is a question in which we are *all* implicated;—we are all guilty,—(with shame and compunction let us admit the opprobrious truth) of supporting and perpetuating slavery. The West Indian planter and the people of this country, stand in the same moral relation to each other, as the thief and the receiver of stolen goods. The planter refuses to set his wretched captive at liberty,—treats him as a beast of burden,—compels his reluctant unremunerated labour under the lash of the cart whip, —why?—because WE furnish the stimulant to all this injustice, rapacity, and cruelty,—by PURCHASING ITS PRODUCE. Heretofore, it may have been thoughtlessly and unconsciously,—but now this palliative is removed;—the veil of ignorance is rent aside;—the whole nation must now divide itself into the *active supporters*, and

the *active opposers* of slavery ;—there is no longer
any ground for a neutral party to stand upon.

The state of slavery, in our West Indian islands,
is now become notorious ;—*the secret is out;*—
the justice and humanity, the *veracity* also, of
slave owners,—is exactly ascertained ;—the credit
due to their assertions, that their slaves are better
fed, better clothed,—are more comfortable, more
happy than our English peasantry, is now universally understood. The tricks and impostures
practised by the colonial assemblies, to hoodwink
the people,—to humbug the Government,—and
to bamboozle the *saints* (as the friends of emancipation are scornfully termed)—have all been detected—and the cry of the nation has been raised,
from one end to the other, against this complicated system of knavery and imposture,—of
intolerable oppression, of relentless and savage
barbarity.

But is all this knowledge to end in exclama-
tions, in petitions, and remonstrances ?—Is there
nothing to be *done*, as well as said ? Are there
no tests to prove our sincerity,—no sacrifices to
be offered in confirmation of our zeal ?—Yes,
there is *one*,—(but it is in itself so small and
insignificant that it seems almost burlesque to
dignify it with the name of sacrifice)—it is ABSTI-

NENCE FROM THE USE OF WEST INDIAN
PRODUCTIONS, *sugar*, especially, in the cultivation of which slave labour is chiefly occupied.
Small, however, and insignificant as the sacrifice
may appear,—it would, at once, give the death
blow to West Indian slavery. When there was
no longer a market for the productions of *slave
labour*, then, and *not till then*, will the slaves be
emancipated.

Many had recourse to this expedient about
thirty years ago, when the public attention was
so generally roused to the enormities of the Slave
Trade. But when the trade was abolished by
the British legislature, it was too readily con-
cluded that the abolition of slavery, in the British
dominions, would have been an inevitable consequence, this species of abstinence was therefore
unhappily discontinued.

" But, (it will be objected) if there be no market for West Indian produce, the West Indian
proprietors will be ruined, and the slaves, instead
of being benefited, will perish by famine." Not
so,—the West Indian proprietors understand their
own interest better. The market though shut to
the productions of *slave labour*, would still be
open to the productions of *free labour*,—and the
planters are not such devoted worshippers of

slavery as to make a voluntary sacrifice of their own interests upon her altar;—they will not doom the soil to perpetual barrenness rather than suffer it to be cultivated by free men. It has been abundantly proved that voluntary labour is more productive,—more advantageous to the employer than compulsory labour. The experiments of the venerable and philanthropic Joshua Steele have established the fact beyond all doubt:—But the planter shuts his eyes to such facts, though clear and evident as the sun at noon day.—None are so blind as those who *will* not see. The conviction then must be *forced* upon these infatuated men. It is often asserted, that slavery is too deeply rooted an evil to be eradicated by the exertions of any principle less potent and active than *self interest*—if so, the resolution to abstain from West Indian produce, would bring this potent and active principle into the fullest operation,—would *compel* the planter to set his slaves at liberty.

But were such a measure to be ultimately injurious to the interest of the planter—that consideration ought not to weigh a feather in the scale against emancipation. The slave has a *right* to his liberty, a right which it is a crime to withhold—let the consequences to the planters be what they may. If I have been deprived of my rightful inheritance, and the usurper, because he has long kept possession, asserts his *right* to the property of which he has defrauded me ;—are my just claims to it at all weakened by the boldness of his pretensions, or by the plea that restitution would impoverish and involve him in ruin? And to what inheritance, or birth-right, can any mortal have pretensions so just, (until forfeited by crime) as to liberty ? What injustice and rapacity can be compared to that which defrauds a man of his best earthly inheritance,—tears him from his dearest connexions, and condemns him and his posterity to the degradation and misery of interminable slavery ?

In the great question of emancipation, the interests of *two* parties are said to be involved,— the interest of the slave and that of the planter. But it cannot for a moment be imagined that these two interests have an equal right to be consulted, without confounding all moral distinctions, all difference between real and pretended, between substantial and assumed claims. With the interest of the planter, the question of emancipation has (properly speaking) nothing to do. The right of the slave, and the interest of the planter, are distinct questions ;—they belong to separate departments, to different provinces of consideration. If the liberty of the slave can be secured not only without injury but with advantage to the planter, so much the better, certainly;—but still the liberation of the slave ought ever to be regarded as an independent object; and if it be deferred till the planter is sufficiently alive to his own interest to co-operate in the measure, we may for ever despair of its accomplishment. The cause of emancipation has been long and ably advocated.—Reason and eloquence, persuasion and argument have been powerfully exerted;—experiments have been fairly made,—facts broadly stated in proof of the impolicy as well as iniquity of slavery,—to little purpose;—even the *hope* of its extinction, with the concurrence of the planter,—or by any enactment of the colonial, or British legislature, is still seen in very remote perspective,—so remote, that the heart sickens at the cheerless prospect. All that zeal and talent could display in the way of argument, has been exerted in vain. All that an accumulated mass of indubitable evidence could effect in the way of conviction, has been brought forward to no effect.

It is high time then, to resort to other measures, — to ways and means more summary and effectual. Too much time has already been lost in declamation and argument, — in petitions and remonstrances against *British* slavery.— The cause of emancipation calls for something more decisive, more efficient than words. It calls upon the real friends of the poor degraded and oppressed African to bind themselves by a solemn engagement, — an irrevocable vow, to participate no longer in the crime of keeping him in bondage. It calls upon them to "wash their own hands in innocency ;" — to abjure for ever the miserable hypocrisy of pretending to commiserate the slave, whilst, by purchasing the productions of his labour they *bribe* his master to keep him in slavery. The great Apostle of the gentiles declared, that he would " eat no flesh whilst the world stood, rather than make his Brother to offend." Do you make a similar resolution respecting West Indian produce. — Let your resolution be made conscientiously, and kept inviolably ;—let no plausible arguments which may be urged against it from without,—no solicitations of appetite from within, move you from your purpose,—and in the course of a few months, slavery in the British dominions will be annihilated.

" Yes, (it may be said) if *all* would unite in such a resolution,—but what can the abstinence of a few individuals, or a few families do, towards the accomplishment of so vast an object?"—It can do wonders. Great effects often result from small beginnings.—Your resolution will influence that of your friends and neighbours ;—each of them will,

in like manner, influence their friends and neighbours ;—the example will spread from house to
house,—from city to city,—till, *among those who
have any claim to humanity*, there will be but one
heart, and one mind,—one resolution,—one uni-
form practice. Thus, *by means the most simple
and easy, would West Indian slavery be most
safely and speedily abolished.*

" But, (it will be objected) it is not an *immediate*, but a *gradual* emancipation, which the
most enlightened and judicious friends of humanity call for, as a measure best calculated, in their
judgment, to promote the real interests of the
slave, as well as his master ; the former, not being
in a condition to make a right use of his freedom,
were it suddenly restored to him." This, it must
be admitted, appears not only the general, but
almost universal sentiment of the abolitionists ;—
to oppose it therefore, may seem a most pre-
sumptuous, as well as hopeless attempt. But
truth and justice are stubborn and inflexible ;—
they yield neither to numbers or authority.

The history of emancipation in St. Domingo,
and of the conduct of the emancipated slaves for
thirty years subsequent to that event (as detailed
in Clarkson's admirable pamphlet, on the necessity of improving the condition of our West Indian

slaves,) is a complete refutation of all the elaborate arguments which have been artfully advanced to discredit the design of *immediate* emancipation. No instance has been recorded in these important annals, of the emancipated slaves, (not the *gradually*, but the *immediately* emancipated slaves) having abused their freedom. On the contrary, it is frequently asserted in the course of the narrative, that the negroes continued to work upon all the plantations as quietly as before emancipation. Through the whole of Clarkson's diligent and candid investigations of the conduct of emancipated slaves, comprising a body of more than 500,000 persons,—under a great variety of circumstances,—a considerable proportion of whom had been *suddenly* emancipated,—*with all the vicious habits of slavery upon them;*—many or them *accustomed to the use of arms*; he has not, throughout this vast mass of emancipated slaves, found a *single instance of bad behaviour*, not even a refusal to work, or of disobedience to orders; much less, had he heard of frightful massacres, or of revenge for past injuries, even when they had it amply in their power. Well might this benevolent and indefatigable abolitionist arrive at the conslusion, " that emancipation, (why did he not say *immediate* emancipation ?) was not only practicable, but practicable without danger." All the frightful massacres and conflagrations which took place in St. Domingo, in 1791 and 1792, *occurred during the days of slavery.* They originated too, not with the slaves, but with the white and coloured planters,—between the royalists, and the revolutionists, who, for purposes of mutual vengeance, called in the aid of the slaves, Colonel Malenfant, in his history of the emancipation, written during his residence in St. Domingo, *ridicules the notion that the negroes would not work without compulsion,*—and asserts, that in one plantation, more immediately under his own observation, on which more than four hundred negroes were employed, *not one in the number refused to work after* their emancipation.

In the face of such a body of evidence, the detaining our West Indian slaves in bondage, is a continued acting of the same atrocious injustice which first kidnapped and tore them from their kindred and native soil, and robbed them of that sacred unalienable right which no considerations, how plausible soever, can justify the withholding. We have no right, on any pretext of expediency or pretended humanity, to say—" because you have been made a slave, and thereby degraded and debased,—therefore, I will continue to hold you in bondage until you have acquired a capacity to make a right use of your liberty." As well might you say to a poor wretch, gasping and languishing

in a pest house, "here will I keep you, till I
have given you a capacity for the enjoyment of
pure air."

You admit, that the *vices* of the slave, as well
as his miseries,—his intellectual and moral, as
well as corporeal degradation are consequent on
his slavery;—remove the cause then, and the
effect will cease. Give the slave his liberty,—in
the sacred name of justice, give it him at once.
Whilst you hold him in bondage, he will profit
little from your plans of amelioration. He has
not, by all his complicated injuries and debase-
ments, been disinherited of his *sagacity*;—this
will teach him to give no credit to your admoni-
tory lessons—your Christian instructions will be
lost upon him, so long as he both knows and feels
that his instructors are grossly violating their
own lessons.

The enemies of slavery have hitherto ruined
their cause by the senseless cry of *gradual* emancipation. It is marvellous that the *wise* and the
good should have suffered themselves to have
been imposed upon by this wily artifice of the
slave holder,—for with him must the project of
gradual emancipation have first originated. The
slave holder knew very well, that his prey would
be secure, so long as the abolitionists could be

cajoled into a demand for *gradual* instead of *immediate* abolition. He knew very well, that the contemplation of a *gradual* emancipation, would beget a *gradual indifference to emancipation itself.* He knew very well, that even the *wise* and the *good,* may, by habit and familiarity, be brought to endure and tolerate almost any thing. He had caught the poet's idea, that—

> " Vice is a monster of such frightful mien,
> " As to be hated, need but to be seen ;
> " But, seen too oft, *familiar with her face,*
> " *We first endure, then pity, then embrace."*

He caught the idea, and knew how to turn it to advantage. — He knew very well, that the faithful delineation of the horrors of West Indian slavery, would produce such a general insurrection of sympathetic and indignant feeling ; such abhorrence of the oppressor, such compassion for the oppressed, as must soon have been fatal to the whole system. He knew very well, that a strong moral fermentation had begun, which, had it gone forward, must soon have purified the nation from this foulest of its corruptions ; — that the cries of the people for emancipation, would have been too unanimous, and too importunate for the Government to resist, and that slavery would, long ago, have been exterminated throughout the British dominions. Our example might have spread from kingdom to kingdom, — from continent to continent, — and the slave trade, and slavery, might, by this time, have been abolished — all the world over : — " A sacrifice of a sweet savour," might have ascended to the Great Parent of the Universe ; — " His kingdom might have come, and his will (thus far) have been done on earth, as it is in Heaven."

But this GRADUAL ABOLITION, has been the grand marplot of human virtue and happiness ;— the very master-piece of satanic policy. By converting the cry for *immediate*, into *gradual* emancipation, the prince of slave holders, " transformed himself, with astonishing dexterity, into an angel of light,"—and thereby—" deceived the very elect."—He saw very clearly, that if public justice and humanity, especially, if *Christian* justice and humanity, could be brought to demand only a *gradual* extermination of the enormities of the slave system ;—if they could be brought to *acquiesce*, but for one year, or for one month, in the slavery of our African brother,—in robbing him of all the rights of humanity,—and degrading him to a level with the brutes ;—that then, they could imperceptibly be brought to acquiesce in all this for an unlimited duration. He saw, very clearly, that the time for the extermination of slavery, was precisely that, when its horrid impiety and enormity were *first distinctly known and strongly felt.* He knew, that every moment's unnecessary delay, between the discovery of an imperious duty, and the setting earnestly about its accomplishment, was dangerous, if not fatal to success. He knew, that strong excitement, was necessary to strong effort;—that intense feeling was necessary to stimulate intense exertion;— that, as strong excitement, and intense feeling are generally transient, in proportion to their strength and intensity,—the most effectual way of crushing a great and virtuous enterprize,—was to gain time,—to defer it to "a more convenient season," when the zeal and ardour of the first convictions of duty had subsided;—when our sympathies had become languid;—when considerations of the difficulties and hazards of the enterprize, the solicitations of ease and indulgence should have chilled the warm glow of humanity,—quenched the fervid heroism of virtue;—when familiarity with relations of violence and outrage, crimes and miseries, should have abated the horror of their first impression, and, at length, induced indifference.

The father of lies, the grand artificer of fraud and imposture, transformed himself therefore, on this occasion, pre-eminently, "into an angel of light"—and deceived, not the unwary only, the unsuspecting multitude,—but the wise and the good, by the plausibility, the apparent force, the justice, and above all, by the *humanity* of the arguments propounded for *gradual* emancipation. He, is the subtlest of all reasoners, the most ingenious of all sophists, the most eloquent of all declaimers.—He, above all other advocates, "can make the worse appear the better argument;" can, most effectually, pervert the judgment and blind the understanding,—whilst they seem to be most enlightened and rectified. Thus, by a train of most exquisite reasoning, has he brought the abolitionists to the conclusion,—that the interest of the poor, degraded, and oppressed *slave*, as well as that of his master, will be best secured by his *remaining in slavery.* It has indeed, been proposed to mitigate, in some degree, the miseries of his interminable bondage, but the blessings of *emancipation*, according to the propositions of the abolitionists in the last session of Parliament, were to be reserved for his *posterity* alone,—and every idea of *immediate* emancipation is still represented, not only as impolitic, enthusiastic and visionary, but as highly injurious to the slave himself,—and a train of supposed apt illustrations is continually at hand, to expose the absurdity of such a project. " Who (it is asked) would place a sumptuous banquet before a half-famished wretch, whilst his powers of digestion were so feeble that it would be fatal to partake of it?—

c

Who would bring a body benumbed and half frozen with cold, into sudden contact with fervid heat? Who would take a poor captive from his dungeon, where he had been immured whole years, in total darkness, and bring him at once into the dazzling light of a meridian sun? No one, in his senses, certainly. All these transitions from famine to plenty,—from cold to heat, —from darkness to light, must be gradual in order to be salutary. But must it therefore follow, by any inductions of common sense, that emancipation out of the gripe of a robber or an assassin,— out of the jaws of a shark or a tiger, must be gradual? Must it, therefore, follow, that the wretched victim of slavery must always remain in slavery?—that emancipation must be *so* gradual, that the blessings of freedom shall never be tasted by him who has endured all the curses of slavery, but be reserved for his posterity alone?

There is something unnatural, something revolting to the common sense of justice, in reserving all the sweets of freedom for those who have never tasted the bitter cup of bondage,—in dooming those who have once been compelled to drink it, to drain it to the very dregs. Common equity demands that relief should be administered first to those who have suffered most;—that the healing balm of mercy should be imparted first to

those who have smarted most under the rod of
oppression ; that those who have borne the galling
yoke of slavery, should first experience the blessings of liberty. The cause of emancipation loses
more than half its interest, when the public
sympathy is diverted from its natural channel,—
turned from the *living* victims of colonial bondage
to their unborn progeny.

It is utterly astonishing, with such an object as
West Indian slavery before us, rendered palpable,
in all its horrors, almost to our very senses, by a
multitude of indubitable facts, collected from
various sources of the highest authority, all uniting
in the same appalling evidence ;—with the sight
of our fellow-creatures in bondage so rigorous,—
in moral and physical degradation so abject ;—
under a tyranny so arbitrary, wanton and barbar-
ous ;—it is utterly astonishing, that our compassion and sympathy should be so timid and
calculating,—so slow and cautious.

Under the contemplation of *individual* suffering, comparatively trifling, both in nature and
duration, our compassion is prompt and quick in
its movements,—our exertions, spontaneous and
instinctive ;—we go the shortest way to work, in
effecting the relief of the sufferer. But, in eman-
cipating *eight hundred thousand* of our fellow

creatures and fellow subjects from a worse than
Egyptian bondage, we advance towards the
object, by a route, the most indirect and circuit-
ous ; we petition Parliament, year after year, for
gradual emancipation :—to what purpose ? Are
we gaining or losing ground by these delays ?
Are we approaching nearer or receding farther
from the attainment of our object ? The latter,
it is too evident, is, and must be the case. The
evil principle is more subtle and active in its
various operations, than the good principle. The
advocates of slavery, are more alert and successful
in insinuating into the public mind, doubts and
fears, coldness and apathy on the subject of emancipation, than the abolitionists are in counter-
acting such hostile influence ;—and the desertions
from the anti-slavery standard in point of zeal and
activity, if not in numbers, since the agitation of
the question in Parliament last year, are doubtless
very considerable.

Should the numerous petitions to Parliament
be ultimately successful ;—should the prayer for
gradual emancipation be granted ; still, how vague
and indefinite would be the benefit resulting from
such success. Should some specific time be
appointed by government, for the final extinction
of colonial slavery ;—that period, we have been
informed from high authority, will not be an early

one. And who can calculate the tears and groans, the anguish and despair;—the tortures and outrages which may be added, during the term of that protracted interval, to the enormous mass of injuries already sustained by the victims of West Indian bondage? Who can calculate the aggravated accumulation of guilt which may be incurred by its active agents, its interested abettors and supporters? Why then, in the name of humanity, of common sense, and common honesty, do we petition Parliament, year after year, for a gradual abolition of this horrid system,—this complication of crime and misery? Why petition Parliament *at all*, to do that for us, which, were they ever so well disposed, we can do more speedily and more effectually for ourselves?

It is no marvel that *slave holders*, should cry out against immediate emancipation, as they have done against all propositions for softening the rigors of colonial slavery. "*Insurrection of all the blacks,—massacre of all the whites,*"—are the bug-bears which have been constantly conjured up, to deter the British Parliament from all interference between the master and his slave. The panic was the same, the outcry just as violent, when an attempt was made about forty years ago, to abate the horrors of the middle passage, by admitting a little more air into the suffocating and pestilent holds of the slave ships; and a noble duke, besought Parliament *not to meddle with the alarming question*[a]. Confident predictions, from this quarter, of rebellion and bloodshed, have, almost uniformly followed every proposition to restrain the power of the oppressor and to mitigate the sufferings of the oppressed.

It is therefore no wonder, that West Indian proprietors, and slave holders, should exclaim against immediate emancipation; that they should tell us, the slaves are so *depraved* as well as degraded, as to be utterly incapacitated for the right use of freedom;—that emancipation, instead of leading them into habits of sober contented industry, would be inevitably followed by idleness, pillage, and all sorts of enormities;—in short, *that they would rise in a mass, and massacre all the white inhabitants of the islands.*

That *slave holders* should say, and really believe all this, is perfectly natural;—it is no wonder at all that they should be full of the most groundless suspicions and terrors;—for tyrants are the greatest of all cowards.—" The wicked fleeth when no man pursueth;"—he is terrified at shadows,—and shudders at the spectres of his own guilty imagination.

---

[a] See the Debate on this subject in 1823.

But that the *abolitionists* should have caught the infection,—should be panic-struck ;—that the friends of humanity,—the wise and the good— should be diverted from their purpose by such visionary apprehensions ;—that they should " fear where no fear is ;"—should swallow the bait, so manifestly laid to draw them aside from their great object ;—that they should be so credulous, so easily imposed upon—is marvellous.

The simple enquiry, what is meant by emancipation? might have dissipated at once all these terrible spectres of rapine and murder. Does emancipation from slavery imply emancipation from law? Does emancipation from lawless tyranny,—from compulsory unremunerated labour. under the lash of the cart whip, imply emancipation from all responsibility and moral restraint? Were slavery in the British colonies extinguished,—the same laws which restrain and punish crime in the *white* population, would still restrain and punish crime in the *black* population. The danger arising from inequality of numbers would be more than counteracted by the wealth and influence, the armed force, possessed by the former. But independent of such considerations, the oppressed and miserable, corrupt as is human nature, do not naturally become savage and revengeful when their oppressions and miseries are

removed. As long as a human being is bought
and sold,—regarded as goods and chattels,—
compelled to labour without wages,—branded,
chained, and flogged at the caprice of his owner;
he will, of necessity, as long as the feeling of
pain,—the sense of degradation and injury remain,
he will, unless he have the spirit of a Christian
martyr, be vindictive and revengeful. " Oppression (it is said) will make (even) a wise man,
mad." But will the liberated captive, when the
iron yoke of slavery is broken ;—when his heavy
burdens are unbound,—his bleeding wounds
healed,—his broken heart bound up ; will he then
scatter vengeance and destruction around him ?

Should the wretched African find the moment
for *breaking his own chains,—and asserting his
own freedom,*—he may well be expected to take
terrible vengeance,—to push the law of retaliation
to its utmost extreme. But, when presented with
his freedom,—when the sacred rights of humanity
are restored to him,—would that be the moment
for rage, for revenge and murder ? To *polished* and
Christianized Europeans, such abuses of liberty
may appear natural and inevitable, since their own
history abounds with them. But the history of
negro emancipation abundantly proves that no
such consequences are to be apprehended from
the poor *uncultivated* and *despised* African.

" But, to demand *immediate* emancipation, however safe, however just and desirable in itself, would (we are told) be most *impolitic*,—for it would never be granted;—by striving to obtain too much, you would lose all. You must go cautiously and gradually to work. A very powerful interest and a very powerful influence are against you. You must try to conciliate instead of provoke the West Indian planters;—to convince them that their own interest is concerned in the better treatment and gradual emancipation of their slaves, or your object will never be accomplished."

But you will strive and labour in vain;—you will reason, however eloquently, however forcibly, in the ears of the " deaf adder." The moral and rational perceptions of the *slave holder*, are still more perverted than those of the slave;—oppression, is more debasing and injurious to the intellect of the oppressor, than that of the oppressed. The gains of unrighteousness,—familiarity with injustice and cruelty, have rendered the slave holder, more obstinately, more incurably blind and inaccessible to reason, than the slave. And what justice or restitution would there be in the world, were unlawful possessions never to be reclaimed till there was a disposition in the possessor *voluntarily* to relinquish them,—till he was convinced that it was his *interest* to part with them?

D

28

The interests and the prejudices of the West Indian planters, have occupied much too prominent a place in the discussion of this great question. The abolitionists have shewn a great deal too much politeness and accommodation towards these gentlemen. With reference to them, the question is said, to be a very *delicate* one. (Was ever the word delicacy so preposterously misapplied?)—It is said, to be beset with difficulties and dangers.—Yes, the parties interested,—*criminally* interested, protest that the difficulties are insurmountable,—the dangers tremendous. But those difficulties and dangers have been proved to be visionary and futile,—the offspring of idle, or of hypocritical fears. A little *temporary* pecuniary loss, would be the mighty amount of all the calamities which emancipation would entail upon its virulent and infuriated opposers.[b] And is that a consideration to stand in competition with the liberation of *eight hundred thousand* of our fellow creatures from the heavy yoke of slavery? Must hundreds of thousands of human beings continue to be disinherited of those inherent rights of humanity, without which, life becomes a curse, instead of a blessing;—must they continue to be roused and stimulated to

[b] The account of the London Meeting of West Indian Planters, which took place in February last, perfectly justifies the application of these epithets.

uncompensated labour, night as well as day, during a great part of the year, by the impulse of the cart whip,—that a few *noble lords* and *honourable gentlemen* may experience no privation of expensive luxury,—no contraction of profuse expenditure,—no curtailment of state and equipage? Must the scale in which is placed the just claims, the sacred rights of *eight hundred thousand British subjects*, be made to kick the beam, when weighed in the balance against pretensions so comparatively light and frivolous?

Among the West Indian proprietors, there are doubtless, individuals of high character and respectability, whose education and circumstances may, nevertheless, disqualify them from taking a strictly impartial view of colonial slavery. Such, of course, must be exempt from the just odium, —the reprobation, which belongs to the general body, as far as they have rendered their own character notorious by their own declarations,— by the speeches they have published, and the decrees they have issued;—by the virulent abuse, the rage and calumny which they have heaped upon the abolitionists;—by the alternations of fawning servility and insolent threatening, with which they at one time " prostrate themselves at the foot of the throne;"—at another, protest, in the tone of defiance, not to say rebellion, against

British interference with colonial legislation.
Towards these gentlemen, there has been extended
a great deal too much delicacy and tenderness.
They are *culprits*, in the strictest sense of the
word,—and as such, they ought to be regarded,
notwithstanding their rank and consequence, by
every honest impartial moralist. They have
received too long, the gains of oppression ;—too
long have they battened on the spoils of humanity.

It matters not at all, how, or when, the planter
acquired his pretended right to the slave ;—whether by violence or robbery,—by purchase or by
inheritance. His claim always was, and always
will be, ill-founded, because it is opposed to
nature, to reason, and to religion. It is also
illegal, as far as legality has any foundation of
justice, divine or human, to rest upon. His plea
for protection against the designs of the abolitionists, on the ground that his property has been
embarked in this nefarious speculation, on the
faith of Parliament,—in the confidence that no
change would be effected in the laws which sanction the enormous injustice and wickedness of
slavery, is childish and futile. Are not commercial speculations of every kind, subject to perpetual vicissitudes and revolutions? Are not
human laws perpetually undergoing new modifications and changes, in accommodation to the

ever-varying circumstances of the times,—to increasing light and civilization? It is absurd to imagine that the progress of humanity, of moral and political improvement, is to be arrested, because some individual perquisites, derived from institutions of brutal ignorance and barbarism, would be curtailed. A great deal more reasonably might the industrious artizan, whose daily subsistence depends on his daily labour,—whose only property is his labour—and who, in many cases, has no means, like the West Indian capitalist, of transferring it from one channel to another;—with a great deal more reason might he exclaim and cry out for protection against all mechanical improvements, which diminish labour, which deprive thousands of the labouring classes of their wonted resources, and drive them to beggary.

But if the West Indian gentlemen fail to obtain *protection* against the designs of the abolitionists, then, they demand *compensation*, in the event of the emancipation of their slaves, to the immense amount of *sixty-four millions*. And is *compensation* demanded in no other quarter?—or, if not demanded, is it no where else due? If compensation be demanded as an act of justice to the slave holder, in the event of the liberation of his slaves;—let justice take her free, impartial course;—let compensation be made in the first instance, where it is most due ;—let compensation be first made to the *slave*, for his long years of uncompensated labour, degradation and suffering. It is in *this* quarter, that justice cries aloud for *compensation*,—and if our attention is turned, but for a moment, to these two substantial and well authenticated claims,—the demands of the *slave holder ;* (even had they been couched in terms less arrogant and insulting,) will become not a little questionable.

Experience has already sufficiently evinced the fallacy of the notion, of the superior *policy* of aiming at gradual, instead of immediate emancipation, on the ground of its meeting with less opposition ; for the planters have shewn themselves just as much enraged at the idea of *gradual*, as of immediate emancipation. They appear indeed, either incapable of perceiving, or determined to confound all distinction between them ;—for, in the bitterness of their invectives, they accuse the *gradual* abolitionists of endeavouring to bring upon their heads all the calamities and destruction which they formerly deprecated as the inevitable consequence of *immediate* emancipation.

On this great question, the spirit of accommodation and conciliation has been a spirit of delusion. The abolitionists have lost, rather than

gained ground by it;—their cause has been
weakened, instead of strengthened. The great
interests of truth and justice are betrayed, rather
than supported, by all softening qualifying con-
cessions. Every iota which is yielded of their
rightful claims, impairs the conviction of their
rectitude, and, consequently, weakens their success. Truth and justice, make their best way in
the world, when they appear in bold and simple
majesty ;—their demands are most willingly con-
ceded, when they are most fearlessly claimed.

Were the *immediate* freedom of the slave
demanded, because, in the first instance, it was
unlawfully and violently wrested from him ;—
because, ever since, it has been most unjustly
and cruelly withheld from him ;—because it
is his unalienable right, which he holds by a
divine charter, which no human claims can dis-
annul :—were the immedaite abolition of slavery,
in the *British dominions*, demanded, because
slavery, is in direct opposition to the spirit of the
British constitution, to the spirit and letter of the
Christian religion,—to every principle of humanity
and justice ;—because, as long as it is suffered to
exist, it must remain the fruitful source of the
most atrocious crimes, the most cruel sufferings ;
—because, as long as it is suffered to exist, its
abettors and supporters, passive as well as active,

(now that their eyes are wide open to its enormi-ties) must lie under the divine malediction, and experience, sooner or later, the certain and awful visitations of retributive justice,—the fearful accomplishment of that solemn declaration,— " With what measure ye mete, it shall be measured to you again :"—Demands so evidently just,—such plain appeals to reason and conscience, —to law and equity ;—such serious reference to Divine authority,—to future retribution ;—would be more successful,—would be better calculated to keep alive the public sympathy,—would lead to more unwearied exertions,—to greater sacrifices,—than the slow, cautious, accommodating measures now proposed by the abolitionists ;— than any timorous suggestions of expediency,— any attempts to conciliate the favour, or to disarm the opposition of West Indian slave holders.

When an obvious and imperative duty is encumbered with considerations which do not properly belong to it ; its obligations, instead of being enforced, are enfeebled ;—its motives, instead of being concentrated, are divided and scattered ; and the duty, if not entirely neglected, will be but languidly and partially performed. We make slow progress in virtue, lose much time and labour, when, instead of going boldly forward in its straight and obvious path, we are continually enquiring how far we may proceed in it without difficulty and without opposition.

Had the abolitionists preserved a single eye to their great object;—had they kept it distinct and separate from all extraneous considerations;—had they pursued it by a course more direct, through means more simple;—had they confided more in the goodness of their cause, and dreaded less the opposition of its adversaries;—had they depended more upon divine, and less upon human support—their triumphs, instead of their defeats, would, long since, have been recorded. Surely their eyes must at length be opened;—they must perceive that they have not gone the right way to work,—that the apprehension of *losing all*, *by asking too much*,—has driven them into the danger of losing all, by having asked *too little;*—that the spirit of compromise and accommodation has placed them nearly in the situation of the unfortunate man in the fable, who, by trying to please every body, pleased nobody, and lost the object of his solicitude into the bargain.

It had been well, for the poor oppressed African, had the asserters of his rights entered the lists against his oppressors, with more of the spirit of· Christian combatants, and less of worldly politicians;—had they remembered, through the whole

E

of the struggle, that it was a conflict of sacred
duty, against sordid interest,—of right against
might;—that it was, in fact, an *holy war*,—an
attack upon the strong holds, the deep intrench-
ments of the very powers of darkness ; in which,
courage would be more availing than caution ;—in
which success wasto be expected, less from pru-
dential or political expedients, than from that all-
controling power, which alone gives efficacy to
human exertions,—which often defeats the best
concerted schemes of human sagacity and accom-
plishes his great purposes through the instrumen-
tality of the simplest agency. Had the labours of the
abolitionists been begun and continued on Divine,
instead of human reliance,—*immediate* emancipation would have appeared just as attainable as
gradual emancipation.   But, by substituting the
latter object for the former, under the idea that its
accomplishment was more probable, less exposed
to objection ;—and by endeavouring to carry it,
through considerations of interest, rather than
obligations of duty ; they have betrayed an unworthy diffidence in the cause in which they have
embarked ;—they have converted the great business of emancipation into an object of political
calculation ;—they have withdrawn it from Divine,
and placed it under human patronage ;—and disappointment and defeat, have been the inevitable
consequence.

If the deadly root of slavery be ever extirpated out of British soil, it will be by such exertions as are prompted by duty rather than interest. We cannot sufficiently admire the great wisdom and goodness of those providential arrangements which have, in the general course of events, so inseperably connected our duty with our interest;—but with regard to the broad and palpable distinctions between right and wrong, virtue and vice;—the more simple and direct the reference to the will of our Divine Lawgiver, and that of his vicegerent, conscience,—the more determined will be our resolution,—the more decisive our conduct.— "How shall I do this great wickedness and sin against God"—will be the most influential of all considerations. And the solemn enquiry, pressed home to the conscience, how an enlightened and Christian government,—how an enlightened and Christian community, can, in any way, encourage or sanction such a complicated system of iniquity as that of slavery,—" the greatest practical blunder, as well as the greatest calamity, that has ever disgraced and afflicted human nature,"—without sharing its guilt, and, if there be a righteous Governer of the universe, its punishment also ?—will be followed up by propositions more consistent and energetic, than such as aim only at its *gradual* extermination.

The very able mover of the question in Parliament last year, proposed that our colonial slavery should be suffered—" to expire of itself,—to die a natural death.—But a natural death, it never will die.—It must be crushed at once, or not at all. While the abolitionists are endeavouring *gradually* to enfeeble and kill it by inches, it will gradually discover the means of reinforcing its strength, and will soon defy all the puny attacks of its assailants.

In the mean time, let the abolitionists remember,—while they are reasoning and declaiming and petitioning Parliament for gradual emancipation,—let them remember, that the miseries they deplore remain unmitigated, — the crimes they execrate are still perpetuated ;—still the tyrant frowns—and the slave trembles ;—the cart-whip still plies at the will of the inhuman driver—and the hopeless victim still writhes under its lash. The ameliorating measures *recommended* by Parliament, to the colonial legislators, are neglected and spurned. The bad passions of the slave holder are exasperated and infuriated by interference, and vengeance falls, with accumulated weight, on the slave. It had been better for him, had no efforts been made for his emancipation, than that they should ultimately fail, or be feebly exerted :—the interval of suspense, will be an interval of restless

perturbation,—of aggravated tyranny in the oppressor,—of aggravated suffering to the oppressed.
*Unsuccessful opposition, to crimes of every de-
scription, invariably increases their power and
malignity.*

An *immediate* emancipation then, is the object
to be aimed at ;—it is more wise and rational,—
more politic and safe, as well as more just and
humane,—than gradual emancipation. The interest, moral and political, temporal and eternal,
of all parties concerned, will be best promoted by
immediate emancipation. The sooner the planter
is obliged to abandon a system which torments
him with perpetual alarms of insurrection and
massacre,—which keeps him in the most debasing
moral bondage,—subjects him to a tyranny, of all
others, the most injurious and destructive—that
of sordid and vindictive passions ;—the sooner he
is obliged to adopt a more humane and more
lucrative policy in the cultivation of his plantations ;—the sooner the over-laboured, crouching
slave, is converted into a free labourer,—his compulsory, unremunerated toil, under the impulse of
the cart whip, exchanged for cheerful, well recom-
pensed industry,—his bitter sufferings for peace-
ful enjoyment,—his deep execration of his merci-
less tyrants, for respectful attachment to his
humane and equitable masters ;—the sooner the

Government and the people of this country purify themselves from the guilt of supporting or tolerating a system of such monstrous injustice, productive of such complicated enormities;—the sooner all this mass of impolicy, crime and suffering is got rid of—the better.

It behoves the advocates of this great cause then, to take the most direct, the most speedy and effectual means of accomplishing their object. If any can be devised more direct, more speedy and effectual, or less exceptionable in its operation than that which has been suggested,—let it be immediately adopted; but let us no longer compromise the requisitions of humanity and justice, for those of an artful and sordid policy;—let there be no betraying of the cause by needless delay;—delay is always dangerous; — on this momentous question, (humanly speaking) it will be fatal, if much longer protracted. The public sympathy is already declining,—people are becoming tired of the subject,—they grow listless and impatient when it is introduced;—they tell you, " they wish to hear no more of it,—their minds are made up,—no advantage can be gained by farther discussion,—the subject must now be left to Parliament." Alas! and *how* has Parliament disposed of it? How has it realized the *very modest* hopes, indulged by the abolitionists,

in consequence of its declarations in favour of
gradual abolition, a year ago ? By its recent decisions, the great work of emancipation appears
to retrograde instead of advance. The bullying of
the slave holders, is said to have proved completely triumphant. The royal proclamation just
issued, is rightly denominated a *hope extinguisher*,
to the wretched slave population. Well may the
abolitionists express their disappointment. on finding the present measures of Government, fall so
far short of the expectations, which the promises
of last session had excited. Well may the right
honourable secretary be charged, with " having
done nothing, or worse than nothing; with being
satisfied, at most, to see his pledge in favour of a
whole archipelago, reduced to a single island ;
while a law is still to prevail in every island of the
West Indies, except *Trinidad*, which authorises a
female negro, to be stripped, in the presence of her
father, husband or son, and flogged with a cart
whip ! !"

There were some, who anticipated these results;
cheerless and melancholy as they are, they are
such as might resonably have been expected from
the proposition for *gradual* emancipation,—and
if persisted in, it will assuredly end, in *no emancipation*. The time is critical. The *general*
interest, in this great subject, is evidently on the

wane,—and it should be remembered, that even
the most humane and susceptible,—those who are
most under the influence of true Christian principle, are not always wound up to such a pitch of
disinterested and ardent zeal, as is requisite to cope
with such a host of interested and powerful opponents, as are the West Indian proprietors and
slave holders. Those, who are " called to glory
and virtue,"—invited, to labour, in the Divine
vineyard,—are admonished, to " work whilst it is
day,—for the night cometh, in which no man can
work;"—whilst they have light, they are admonished to " walk in the light, lest darkness come
upon them." Mental darkness, and spiritual
night, steal fast upon those, who, when an imperious duty is presented to them,—when sufficient
ability is imparted for its accomplishment,—falter
and procrastinate.

If the great work of emancipation be not *now*
accomplished,—humanly speaking, it may be
despaired of, as far as our agency is concerned.
The rising generation may furnish no such zealous, devoted advocates, as a Clarkson, a Wilberforce, and a Buxton. If the clear light, the full
information, they have so generally diffused :—the
deep interest and sympathy they have so generally
excited, produce no other results than those at
present contemplated by the abolitionists ;—this

country may fall under the curse of being judicially hardened and blinded, in consequence of having been softened and enlightened to so little purpose ;—and the emancipation of *eight hundred thousand British slaves!* may be effected through other means and other agency, which, when once roused into action, may realize all those terrific scenes of insurrection and carnage which the imagination of the planter has so often contemplated.

Since the preceding pages were written, the sentences passed upon the insurgents of Demerara and Kingston have reached us. Some, had been hung, others, had received corporeal punishment— to what extent—let those who have ears to hear, and hearts to feel, deeply ponder. Some had received, others, were yet to receive—ONE THOUSAND LASHES,—AND WERE CONDEMNED TO BE WORKED IN CHAINS DURING THE RESIDUE OF THEIR LIVES!! The horrid work, has probably, by this time been completed, human interposition therefore, with respect to these individual victims of WEST INDIAN JUSTICE will now be of no avail.

But shall such sentences as these, be suffered to pass the ordeal of public opinion ? Shall they

F

be established as precedents for future judgments, on future insurgents ? Forbid it—every feeling of humanity—in *every bosom*. Let every principle of virtue which distinguishes the human from the brute creation,—the professors of the benignant, compassionate religion of Christ, from the savage and blood-thirsty worshippers of Moloch,—raise one united, determined and solemn protest against the repetition of these barbarities, which blaspheme the sacred name of justice,—and seem to imprecate Almighty vengeance.

Will the inhabitants of this benevolent, this *Christian* country, *now* want a stimulant to rouse their best exertions,—to nerve their resolutions against all participation with these human blood-hounds ? Will the British public *now* want a " spirit stirring" incentive to prohibit, and to interdict,—henceforth, and for ever,—the merchandize of slavery ? Let the produce of slave labour,—henceforth, and for ever,—be regarded as *" the accursed thing,"* and refused admission into our houses ;—or let us renounce our Christian profession, and disgrace it no longer, by a selfish, cold-hearted indifference, which, under such circumstances, would be reproachful to savages.

What was the offence which brought down this frightful vengeance on the heads of these devoted

victims? What horrible crime could have instigated man, to sentence his fellow man, to a punishment so tremendous?—to doom his brother to
undergo the protracted torture of a THOUSAND
LASHES?—to have his quivering flesh mangled
and torn from his living body?—and to labour
through life, under the galling and ignominious
weight of chains? It was insurrection. But in
what cause did they become insurgents? Was it
not in that cause, which, of all others, can best
excuse, if it cannot *justify* insurrection? Was it
not in the cause of self-defence from the most
degrading, intolerable oppression?

But what was the *immediate* occasion of this
insurrection? What goaded these poor wretches
on to brave the dreadful hazards of rebellion?
One of them, now hanging in chains at Demerara, was sold and separated from his wife and
family of ten children, after a marriage of eighteen
years,—*and thereby made a rebel.* Another was
a slave of no common intellect, whose wife, the
object of his warmest affections, was torn from his
bosom, and forced to become the mistress of an
overseer. His domestic happiness thus destroyed
for ever, he became, (how should it have been
otherwise?) disaffected and desperate. Such pro-
vocations, added to their common and every day
wrongs, seem beyond human endurance, and
might instigate " the very stones to mutiny."

How preposterously partial and inconsistent are we in the extension of our sympathy, our approbation and our assistance towards the oppressed and miserable! We extol the resistance of the *Greeks*,—we deem it heroic and meritorious. We deem it an act of virtue,—of *Christian charity*, to supply *them* with *arms* and *ammunition*, to enable them to *persist in insurrection*. Possibly, in the long list of munificent subscribers to these *Greek* insurgents, the names of some noble lords and honourable gentlemen may be found— who sanction and approve the visitation of WEST INDIAN SLAVE INSURGENTS, with the GIBBET, and the infliction of ONE THOUSAND LASHES!!

But let us, whose moral perceptions are unblinded by interest or prejudice,—whose charity is unwarped by partiality or hypocrisy;—let *us* pursue a more rational and consistent course. Let us not overlook our own urgent duties in the pursuit of such as are less imperative. Let us *first—mind our own business*,—" pluck the beam out of our own eye." Let us *first*, extend the helping hand, to those who have the *first* claim to our assistance. Let us *first*, liberate our own slaves—which we may do, without furnishing them with *arms* or *ammunition*. *Then*, we shall have *clean hands*,—and the Divine blessing may *then* be expected to crown our exertions for the redemption of other captives.

Should the weak objection, still haunt some inconsiderate reader, of the little good, which can reasonably be expected to result from *individual* abstinence from West Indian produce; let him reflect, that the most wonderful productions of human skill and industry; the most astonishing effects of human power, have been accomplished by combined exertions, which, when individually and seperately considered, appear feeble and insignificant. Let him reflect, that the grandest objects of human observation, consist of small agglomerated particles;—that the globe itself, is composed of atoms too minute for discernment; that extended ages, consist of accumulated moments. Let him reflect, that greater victories have been achieved by the combined expression of *individual opinion*, than by fleets and armies;—that greater moral revolutions have been accomplished by the combined exertion of *individual resolution*, than were ever effected by acts of Parliament.

The hydra-headed monster of slavery, will never be destroyed by other means, than the united expression of *individual opinion*, and the united exertion of *individual resolution*. Let no man restrain the expression of the one, or the exertion of the other, from the apprehension that his single efforts will be of no avail. The greatest and the best work must have a *beginning*,—often it is a very small and obscure one. And though the example in question, should not become *universal*, we may surely hope that it will become general.

The great object of emancipation, would probably be effected by the abstinence of less than one-third of the inhabitants of this country. It is too much, to expect that the matter will be taken up—(otherwise, than to make a jest of it)—by the thoughtless and the selfish :—what proportion these bear to the considerate and the compassionate, remains to be ascertained. By *these*, we may reasonably expect that it *will* be taken up, with resolution and consistency. By Christian societies of every denomination,—preeminently by that, which has hitherto stood foremost in the great cause of abolition. By the great body of the Catholics too, who attach so *much merit* to abstinence and self-denial ;—and by all the different Protestant professors, (who are at all sincere in their profession) of the one religion of universal compassion ;—which requires us " *to love our neighbour as ourselves*,"—this testimony against slavery, may be expected to be borne with scrupulous and conscientious fidelity.

Think, but for a moment, at what a trifling sacrifice the redemption of *eight hundred thousand of our fellow creatures from the lowest condition of degradation and misery may be accomplished.*

Abstinence from *one single article* of luxury
would annihilate West Indian slavery!! But
abstinence, it cannot be called;—we only need
substitute *East* India, for *West* India sugar,—and
the British atmosphere would be purified at once,
from the poisonous infection of slavery. The
antidote of this deadly bane; for which we have
been so many years in laborious but unsuccessful
search, is most simple and obvious,—too simple
and obvious, it should seem, to have been regarded. Like Naaman, of old, who expected to
be cured of his leprosy, by some grand and astonishing evolution, and disdained to wash, as he
was directed, in the obscure waters of Damascus;
—we look for the abolition of British slavery, not
to the simple and obvious means of its accomplishment, which lie within our own power,—
but through the slow and solemn process of Parliamentary discussion,—through the " pomp and
circumstance" of legislative enactment;—most
absurdly remonstrating and petitioning *against*
that system of enormous wickedness, which we
voluntarily tax ourselves to the annual amount of
two millions sterling, to *support!!*[c]

That abstinence from West Indian sugar alone,
would sign the death warrant of West Indian

[c] Every reader may not be aware, that such is the amount of
duty laid on *East* India, to keep up the unnatural price of *West*
India sugar.

slavery, is morally certain. The gratuity of two millions annually, is acknowledged by the planters, to be insufficient to bolster up their tottering system,—and they scruple not, to declare to Parliament, that they must be ruined, if the protecting duties, against East India competition, be not augmented.

One, concluding word, to such as may be convinced of the duty, but may still be incredulous as to the *efficacy* of this species of abstinence, from the apprehension that it will never become sufficiently general to accomplish its purpose. Should your example *not* be followed ;—should it be utterly unavailing towards the attainment of its object;—still, it will have its own abundant reward;—still. it will be attended with the consciousness of sincerity and consistency,—of possessing " *clean hands*,"—of having " no fellowship with the workers of iniquity ;"—still, it will be attended with the approbation of conscience,— and doubtless, with that of the Great Searcher of hearts,—who regarded with favourable eye, the mite, cast by the poor widow, into the treasury,— and declared, that a cup of cold water only, administered in Christian charity, " shall in no wise lose its reward."

LEICESTER:
Printed by Thomas Combe.

COMPULSORY MANUMISSION.

COMPULSORY MANUMISSION;

OR

AN EXAMINATION

OF

THE ACTUAL STATE

OF THE

WEST INDIA QUESTION.

BY

ALEXANDER M'DONNELL, Esq.

LONDON:

JOHN MURRAY, ALBEMARLE-STREET

MDCCCXXVII.

LONDON:
PRINTED BY WILLIAM CLOWES,
Stamford-Street.

ADVERTISEMENT.

It is fearful odds against a writer, when, at each stage of his task, he is liable to encounter prejudice as an upholder of a condition of society so repugnant to the feelings of Englishmen as that of slavery.

Greatly must those odds be increased, if a disposition be shown by Government, hitherto believed impartial, to array the weight of its authority against him.

But it is hoped that prejudice will not preclude inquiry. In the following pages it will be found, that in setting forth the actual state of the West India Question, the real and permanent welfare of the slaves occupies a conspicuous place.

In regard to the display of power, let us conclude, that when a measure can be demonstrated as positively bad, such disapprobation will be manifested by the independent and disinterested members of the legislature, as must exercise a salutary control over the counsels of ministers.

Under this impression, the following pages are respectfully submitted to the consideration of the members of both Houses of Parliament.

CONTENTS.

COMPULSORY MANUMISSION.

CHAPTER I.

WEST INDIA PARTY DISINGENUOUSLY TREATED.

THE West India Question is gradually narrowing to a point. There seems now to be little difference of opinion in regard to all safe and practicable measures tending to ameliorate the condition of the slaves, though the time and manner of their adoption may be dependent upon local considerations.

The question of emancipation, or that measure commonly designated Compulsory Manumission, alone remains at issue. The paramount importance of this clause, and the alarm felt in every West India colony at the threat of government to enforce its adoption, has caused the proceedings of the colonial department to be closely scrutinized, and it has in a variety of publications been charged with precipitation.

A pamphlet has lately appeared in vindication, under the title of " Remarks on an Address to the " Members of the New Parliament. on the Pro-

B

·" ceedings of the Colonial Department with respect
" to the West India Question." It is avowedly
" written by a Member of the late Parliament,"
and bears internal evidence of being the production
of a gentleman connected with the Colonial Office.

This pamphlet calls for a reply, for two reasons :
First, because the writer indulges in recrimination,
and brings accusations against the West India
body, which, if passed unnoticed, might produce a
very erroneous impression on the minds of the mo-
derate and disinterested portion of the legislature.

Secondly, because the writer discusses the compulsory manumission clause, and acquaints us with
the nature and strength of the reasoning employed
by government to justify the adoption of that
measure.

The general tone of the publication will create
much surprise, and in one respect it will be of ser-
vice, in making known the true relations and influence of the contending parties. It has been
asserted by the anti-colonial advocates, and be;
lieved by a large portion of the community, that
the West Indians possessed great influence with
government, by means of which their cause was
powerfully strengthened.

If the well-informed portion of the public could
once have entertained this belief, their error must
appear manifest on a perusal of the pamphlet in
question. The writer expresses himself very un-

ceremoniously towards those of the West India body, who were members of the last parliament; and his tone might lead one to conclude that he thinks them not worth conciliation. He seems to justify his asperity, by complaining that the colonial department is improperly singled out for attack in regard to those proceedings which the colonial interests do not approve. Now he must be aware that, constitutionally speaking, *responsibility* peculiarly attaches to that officer of the crown from whose department particular acts ema nate. If important measures affecting the colonies are carried into effect, while there is reason to believe that the Secretary of State for that department is in possession of despatches, official reports, or other information showing their inexpediency, he will be chiefly looked to for the consequences; because it is conceived to be his immediate duty to give full explanation of the details, both to his colleagues and to parliament, and not to incur responsibility for measures he could not conscientiously approve. These are rather the sentiments of the British nation than of any individual party.

It cannot, therefore, be invidious to canvass freely the acts of that particular department. It is the obvious and the regular course where grievances are felt ; and all our ideas of public principle warrant a belief, that when such grievances are fairly stated, every officer of the crown to whose department they referred, so far from feeling indignant at their exposition, would be anxious to extend his protection, in order to have them promptly redressed.

Thus viewing the case, our advocate of the colonial department cannot mistake the tendency or application of any of the comments contained in this publication ; and he will be aware that a fair spirit of argument alone influences an examination of his positions, and of the judgment evinced in the manner and tone with which he has maintained them.

This writer endeavours to defend government, by charging the West Indians with inconsistency. This mode of argument, so frequently resorted to in political warfare, in nine cases out of ten indicates a feeble cause. It can surely never be too late to correct a principle radically wrong.

But let us examine the charge.

It is contended, that compulsory manumission was clearly laid down in the proceedings of parliament in March, 1824; that it was heard by the West India members without opposition, which was an implied acquiescence ; and that if they now turn round to oppose it, they must have been " the most " ignorant, incautious, and imbecile body of men " who ever were got together to represent an in- " terest."

It was well known to the writer of this sentence, that the West India members were unanimously opposed to compulsory manumission ; and it may be added, that a charge, couched in such language as this, could not have been expected from such a quarter. It may be true, that the West India members did not appeal to the House so early or so often as the threatened injustice may have demanded. But is this difficult to account for? When West India members have come forward to state their case, have we not seen it retorted upon them in the widely-disseminated publications of the anti-colonial party, in terms of the utmost coarseness : " He is a slave-driver : what attention or confidence is due to the statement of such a character ?"

The West India members are indeed in a dilemma : if they speak, they run the risk of being abused—if silent, they are to be held parties to all the acts of precipitation and folly which may take place in colonial government.

It would be unnecessary to touch upon this point, did not one remark pre-eminently suggest itself for grave consideration. Throughout this pamphlet we have the defending of parties, clashing of interests, and such terms ; just as if the " Saints" and the West Indians were to fight the battle betwixt them, and whichever proved the most cunning, or the most persevering, would carry their point. And is this the language an apologist of government thinks it necessary to maintain ? Can he have forgotten the grounds on which the West Indians were induced to commit their cause to the care of government ? It was to stop useless or violent discussion. It proceeded from the principle, that if one party declaimed about alleged oppression of the negroes, and the other about their property, the safety of the colonies was the immediate province of ministers ; that, as public servants, it was their sacred duty to uphold all the possessions of the crown ; and that, in watching over their welfare, they equally protected the property of the colonists.

Though this consideration influenced the conduct of many West India members, still it is very erroneous to assert, that no explicit opposition was made to compulsory manumission at the very outset. It is asserted that it passed without animadversion, *" except in a speech* of the present Lord Seaford (Mr. " C. R. Ellis), made on the day on which Mr. " Canning uttered his celebrated commentary on " its enactments." One would think that dissent could not well be more clearly avowed than from the lips of the Chairman of the West India body. In point of fact, sufficient opposition, consistently with the respect which was shown to government, was evinced, to prove that the measure of compulsory manumission was from first to last peculiarly condemned by the colonial interests. When Mr. Canning first made known the intentions of government on this point, Lord Seaford explicitly denied being a party to them. When Mr. Brougham

brought forward his last motion on the same subject, Lord Seaford again gave his reasons for re-
sisting the measure. To those reasons, not a syl-
lable in refutation was offered by Mr. Canning.

Besides these declarations of the chairman, every
West India petition presented either to the king, to
parliament, or to the Colonial office, explicitly set
forth similar sentiments. The agents for the colonies, the merchants and mortgagees, early felt
alarm; and in a petition from these last, presented on the 26th April, 1826, to the Lords
by Lord Redesdale, and to the Commons by Mr.
Baring, it was stated, " That until it shall be
" proved, that free negroes will work for hire, the
" process of compulsory emancipation cannot even
" be experimentally commenced, upon a West
" India estate, with justice to the various parties
" holding legal claims upon the property."

Surely nothing could be more explicit than this,
to convey the opinion of the parties most deeply interested in the question. But the hardy assertion
of the writer we have quoted, calls for still further
explanation. This writer must know, that in every
interview or communication with the Colonial office,
those of the West India body, to whose opinions
most weight was likely to be attached, were loud
and strenuous in their entreaties for forbearance.
They stated, that the government had not given
sufficient examination to the case; that they were

ignorant of many important local circumstances that those ought all first to be carefully and fully investigated before a measure of vital importance was enforced ; and that, in short, the government were already getting into difficulties, and if they proceeded further they would get more deeply involved, and might find it unpleasant, if not impossible, to extricate themselves.

To attempt, therefore, to criminate the West India party, if opposition be now manifested, is not consistent with that impartiality which we have a right to expect from a member of the legislature ; still less does it indicate the manly candour presumed to influence the conduct of an officer of His Majesty's government.

It is argued, again, that a general declaration of dissent was not sufficient. The Order in Council for Trinidad contained four clauses, showing how compulsory manumission was to be carried into execution. That Order was uniformly described as the model for the rest of the colonies ; and it was the duty of the West India party, in their subsequent proceedings, to move for the rescission of those clauses, if they entertained objections to them as a model.

Two reasons may be assigned why the colonists deemed it unnecessary to express their disapproval of the Trinidad order. First, the tenure on which property was held in the British colonies differed from that of the Spanish colony of Trinidad. Secondly, it was notorious, that various portions of that order had to be repeatedly sent home for explanation and remodelling. Was there, then, fair reason to believe, that every clause contained in the original order would be enforced upon the other colonies, while it was yet doubtful if they would be finally confirmed even in the colony for which the order had been originally framed?

Time was afforded the government for reflection. It was presumed, that they would learn, by experience, the difficulty occasioned by legislating precipitately for distant settlements. This line of conduct was dictated by respect for the government. Had the West India body in England come forward in a bolder manner than they had done to resist the determination avowed by the Colonial Secretary of State, how would they have been met? They would have been told by the very same parties who are now wilfully misinterpreting their quiescence—" You are exciting the colonial assemblies to needless opposition—your violence will engender contumacy in its worst form —remain silent till you know what is their decision."

Such reflections undoubtedly did actuate them; but now, when opposition to compulsory manumission is known to be unanimous throughout the colonies which possess legislatures, the West India

body in England, since repeated warnings and
admonitions have been vain, do but consistently
follow them up by appealing in a determined
manner to parliament, and to the British nation,
against the threatened intentions of government
to enforce its enactment.

All the apologists of the measure seem, in their
very tone, to be aware of the great degree of responsibility to be incurred in carrying it into
effect; and hence there is a laboured attempt to
show, that it is strictly conformable with the first
proceedings of parliament, and with the resolutions
of 1823. The West Indians are told, " in addition
to your ignorance and imbecility, there will be the
charge of shameful inconsistency to bring against
you, if you now oppose our measures. You con-
curred unanimously in Mr. Canning's resolutions;
compulsory manumission is distinctly contemplated
by those resolutions ; and can you now propose to
retract the assent given to them by your former
votes."

The West India members had little right to
expect that such an accusation would ever be
brought against them. In every stage of the proceedings, the whisper was incessantly reiterated
in the ear of His Majesty's ministers—" Adhere
honestly to your own resolutions—for the sake of
justice we call upon you, not to court a vulgar
and transient popularity at our expense!"

bi. And why was it that the resolutions were thus implicitly relied on? Not from any opinion that declarations of separate branches of the legislature could affect the rights of individuals resting on the statute-laws of the realm, but, because the parliamentary resolution contained a principle of cautious and practical legislation, and authorised the belief that, at each stage of procedure, careful examination and scrutiny would precede the adoption of measures which could be alleged, by any party concerned, to infringe their rights or interests.

When, subsequently, statements were made in the House of Commons, that government was departing from this principle, in enforcing compulsory manumission, neither Mr. Canning, nor Mr. Wilmot Horton, thought proper openly to attempt an explicit refutation.

What is the commentary? Matters are now becoming more critical, and the Executive resort to the plea of acting only upon the declared will of the legislature in their justification. Let us give them every advantage. Let us discuss the propriety of compulsory manumission, as it agrees with the resolutions of parliament; and if we succeed in our endeavours, we shall command the more attention, from meeting our antagonists on the ground they have themselves selected.

Chapter II.

COMPULSORY MANUMISSION CONTRARY TO THE SPIRIT OF THE RESOLUTIONS OF PARLIAMENT.

The first of these often-quoted Resolutions declares, " That it is expedient to adopt effectual " and decisive measures for AMELIORATING the " condition of the slave population in His Majesty's " colonies."

It was to facilitate the accomplishment of this object of amelioration *alone,* that many respectable West India planters in England gave their sanction to the resolution ; and it is proper here to state, that their interference and acquiescence was by no means of that sweeping character claimed for it by Earl Bathurst in his despatches to the colonies. They explicitly declared, that in none of their proceedings had they the intention of imposing restraints or difficulties upon the colonial legislatures.

The Second Resolution is, " That through a " determined and persevering, but at the same time "judicious and temperate, enforcement of such " measures, this House looks forward to a pro-" gressive improvement in the character of the " slave population, such as may PREPARE them for " a participation in those civil rights and privileges

"which are enjoyed by other classes of His Ma
"jesty's subjects."

This resolution is the one which the writer, who
has undertaken to illustrate the views of government, quotes as decisive of the case. He says,
the object was "'to adopt,'—aye, not only ' to
" adopt,' but ' enforce ' such measures ' in a deter-
" mined and persevering, though at the same time
"judicious and temperate manner,' as would effect,
" —what purpose?—the mitigation of the evils of
" slavery?—as would remove the odious imputa-
" tion of inhumanity adhering to the West Indian
"planters, so generally prevalent at that time
" throughout England, whether true or false? *No :*
" to enforce such measures as might ' prepare them
" for a participation in those civil rights and privi-
" leges which are enjoyed by other classes of His
" Majesty's subjects.' "

The writer here deems contingent emancipation
to be broadly and unequivocally provided, and
in a very triumphant tone, he adds, " What! was
" the intellect of the West Indian members of
" the House of Commons who were present on
" that day, so obtuse, that they could not under-
" stand the meaning of those words ? "

Perhaps not, to answer the ideas of this writer ;
but it is to be hoped that the case will be different
with the legislature at large. It is surely quite
apparent, that if by this Resolution any legislative

measure for effecting emancipation had been contemplated, the term should be, " ADMIT them to
" a participation in civil rights."

The colonial advocate argues throughout upon
this most erroneous assumption. The word " prepare" cannot here admit of two meanings; it is
precise, definite, and strictly accordant with the
desideratum avowed in the first resolution. It was
not possible to convey in a more explicit manner
the obvious fact, that the slaves *are not as yet in a
state to receive freedom*. By " preparing them," it
was understood that they had a probation to go
through ; that their condition had to be materially
changed and improved ; that, in fine, the fruits of
amelioration must have been made visible before further measures were adopted. May we not
ask whether this Second Resolution be not as consistently applicable to the progress which *voluntary*
manumissions are making towards an extinction
of slavery, as to any measure of compulsory manumission? In the one case, as in the other, is it not
expedient to adopt such measures of amelioration,
as may effect a progressive improvement in the
character of the slave population, and PREPARE
them for a participation in those civil rights and
privileges which are enjoyed by other classes of
His Majesty's subjects ?

What, let us demand, was the object of all the
powerful and extensive means taken to secure

moral and religious instruction—of the appointment of the bishops and regular clergy? What was it but to enable the negroes to appreciate correctly the possession of civil privileges, in order that hereafter we might have civilized beings, and not barbarians, living in freedom in our colonies?

But if there could be the least ground for misinterpretation in the Second, it must be speedily removed by attending to the Third Resolution: " That this House is anxious for the accomplish-" ment of this purpose at the earliest period that " shall be compatible with the well-being of the " slaves themselves, with the safety of the colonies, " and with a fair and equitable consideration of the " interests of private property."

Here are laid down certain conditions which must be complied with in whatever new measures are introduced. These conditions constitute the strong reliance of the colonists for protection, since the letter of them definitely confirms what appears to be the spirit of the two preceding Resolutions.

It may be proper to add that, besides the direct declaration of these Resolutions, we have them corroborated by the collateral authority of ministers. In the debate in 1823, Mr. Canning not only made no sort of allusion to compulsory manumission, but that project does not appear to have been even thought of. The mode of emancipation contended for by the anti-colonial party had for its

object the freedom of the rising generation of negroes ; but Mr. Canning both resisted this, and appeared anxious to check any notion which might
be entertained, that plans for emancipation of any
kind were then in contemplation.

As a further and conclusive proof that compulsory manumission was not, even by ministers
themselves, deemed to be implied in the Resolutions proposed by Mr. Canning, but that it was an
after-thought of their own, we have the direct and
decisive testimony of Lord Bathurst.

In his Lordship's circular despatch to the Governors of Colonies having local legislatures, dated
9th July, 1823, and consequently near two months
after these Resolutions were passed, and when it
is presumed that the executive government had determined on the details of such measures as were
to be adopted in furtherance of those Resolutions,
Lord Bathurst gives a comprehensive sketch of the
various amendments required in the colonial laws.

" The next subject," says his Lordship, " to
" which I must draw your attention, is the manu-
" mission of slaves. "

After expressing his satisfaction, that the practice of impeding manumission by the exaction of a
heavy fine or tax has been discontinued, his Lordship anticipates a further facilitation to manumissions, by the concurrence of each colonial legislature in the final repeal of all such charges, includ-

ing all official fees. His Lordship thus appears to consider the *expense* of obtaining emancipation, as the chief obstacle which it was incumbent upon the colonial legislatures to remove.

He then proceeds to specify all the remaining obstacles which he thinks ought to be removed.

" The first obstacle to manumission arises from the apprehension of this being resorted to by the owner for the purpose of relieving himself from the burden of maintaining infirm or aged slaves.—A second obstacle to manumission seems to arise from a presumed legal difficulty, in regard to the incapability of a slave to make contracts.—A third, and much more serious obstacle arises out of the legal limitations to property in slaves ; as in cases of entail, family-settlement, or mortgage.—A difficulty analogous to this arises out of doubtful or disputable titles."

How were these difficulties to be obviated ? By the *compulsory* enactments of the Trinidad order in council? No such thing. They were not even contemplated.

" To remove," says his Lordship, " all the pre-
" ceding obstacles to manumission, you will there-
" fore propose to the legislature of your colony to
" pass a law to the following effect :—Permanent
" commissioners should be appointed, who (on
" application being made by, or on behalf of,
" any slave, *with his master's consent*) should as-

c

" certain the names," &c. &c. Parl. Pap. *Sess.*
1824. p. 10.   ısM

This passage attracted much attention in the colonies. The Court of Policy in Demerara, in stating,
at a subsequent period, that it could not enact compulsory manumission, since " It had not the right
" to invade the property of its fellow-colonists, by
" admitting that they can in any manner be deprived
" of it contrary to the laws by which it is secured
" to them," remarked—" This principle is laid
" down in Earl Bathurst's letter of the 9th July,
" 1823, wherein *the consent of the master* is distinctly
" coupled with the application to be made by or on
" the behalf of a slave for freedom."

This reply of the court of policy of Demerara is
copied into a pamphlet, entitled, " The West India
" Question practically considered," with which per-
formance the Colonial Department may possibly be
acquainted. It has the important words, " consent
" of the master," printed as above in italics, as if to
remind the government more forcibly of its own
previous statement.

After this exposition, may we not venture to ask,
who most deserves the reprobation of disinterested
members of the legislature? The ministerial advocate, who asserts that compulsory manumission
was avowed from the outset, or the West Indian
who can produce Lord Bathurst's own words to
prove the contrary?

It must have been between July, 1823, and March, 1824, that the innovation was devised. But even at the latter period its bearings were not developed.

Few members of the House of Commons can have forgotten Mr. Canning's luminous oration on this occasion, when he described the evil consequences of precipitation, and the difficulties which opposed themselves to the termination of a state like that of slavery.

It is not a little singular, that the same passage which the apologist of the Colonial office quotes from this speech as proving that emancipation was then contemplated, may, with far more effect, be turned against him. Adverting to the other measures of amelioration, Mr. Canning, on the 16th March, 1824, observed: "By this process, and by these " degrees, may the slave be gradually fitted for the " last grand consummation of benefit, the power of " acquiring his freedom."

The term here used, FITTED FOR, is in strict consonance with the word PREPARE, employed by Mr. Canning in the outset; and though he now, for the first time, notices Compulsory Manumission, he passes it over in a very cursory manner, either as if anxious to avoid discussion, or desirous of concealing its importance. An ordinary observer, on reading the more recent despatches sent out to the colonies, in which the views of government were stated, would imagine that, in place of the guarded expressions originally used, terms impelling to quicker and more extensive proceedings had since been substituted.

Consistency is a delicate word to political ears. Lest any misunderstanding should arise, or any member of the legislature should conceive himself shackled by former votes, it was necessary to explain fully to which side the charge attaches of having abandoned former principles.

Having therefore removed that injurious bias which it appears to be the object of the advocate of the Colonial Department to raise against the West Indians, on the ground of inconsistency, it now becomes desirable to discuss the principle of compulsory manumission on its own merits.

It will be found that the opposition of the West Indians is not directed against an imaginary evil; that opposition now is very different from those minor objections locally entertained against particular plans of amelioration ; and that, above all, if government, with a view of courting popular favour, have innovated upon their original understanding with the West Indian party, they have neither chosen the most benevolent nor the wisest mode to accomplish their own end of terminating slavery.

We propose to pursue the examination upon the

grounds marked out by the Parliamentary Resolutions already quoted, in the order in which the importance of the several heads may be presumed to receive attention from a legislative assembly.

1. Justice, as regards the right of property.

2. Humanity, as regards the well-being of the negroes.

3. Sound Policy, as regards the safety of the Colonies.

Chapter III.

INFRINGEMENT OF THE RIGHT OF PROPERTY

Loss of property may be brought upon the Proprietor of a West India estate in two ways:

First, By introducing a new tone of feeling among the Negroes, and converting good servants into bad.

Secondly, By abstracting such a number of efficient hands from an estate, that the remainder are incompetent to carry on its cultivation in an effective manner, or to render its fixed capital productive.

Section 1.

THE CONVERSION OF GOOD SERVANTS INTO BAD.

If we imagine an estate, with a given number of negroes, to produce three hundred hogsheads of sugar a-year, few will be inclined to doubt the disposition of the proprietor to increase its production, if practicable, to three hundred and fifty or four hundred. What are the means, then, to effect this object, without increasing the number of labourers? The proprietor finds himself possessed of a number of people, the development of whose full capability for labour depends upon their treatment.

If they are prompted to work with willingness and satisfaction, skill in the various branches of work to be performed speedily displays itself. If thus some of the slaves can be converted from ordinary labourers into good tradesmen, and if those in the field can be taught to use their utmost dexterity in field-cultivation, a much more profitable division of labour than hitherto will be accomplished. Through this improvement there is less expense in superintendence, there is more work procured from the steady government of the negroes without rigorous coercion, and the cultivation is extended generally, from a better and more skilful distribution of the various employments on the estate.

To accomplish this condition of things, the proprietor is induced to grant to the slaves every reasonable indulgence and benefit. He uses a discriminating power, bestowing reward upon the well-deserving, and withholding it from the vicious ; and thus holds up a double example to the rest.

On the other hand, the slaves, finding that the master deals out his favour with strict impartiality, are cheered under their labour by the assurance that their exertions will be appreciated, and emulate each other in assiduity and good conduct.

It is perfectly evident, therefore, that it is the first interest of the master to have the minds of his people easy and contented ; and that whatever tends to destroy their tranquillity occasions to him inevitable loss of property. He will not then be able to avail himself of that skill and willingness to work above described, and instead of having his three hundred hogsheads increased to four, which he might otherwise have expected from the greater diffusion of intelligence among the rising generation, he will have his produce diminished to two hundred, and rendered still less and less, as discontent spreads and becomes more deeply rooted among his people.

It is one of the worst features of compulsory manumission, that it must inspire this discontent. Is it surprising, therefore, that it should excite such strenuous opposition? The colonists know well, that there is not an instance in our colonies of free negroes working steadily in the field for hire; and that if their people be compulsorily freed, the cultivation of their estates must be superseded. There will no longer be a motive for the master, as at present, to bestow benefits upon the slave; on the contrary, every indulgence granted would only tend to swell that sum which is ultimately to be employed to the master's injury. The negroes will learn, that benefits must cease to flow to them from their masters: hence the interests of the two, instead of being reciprocal as hitherto, become directly opposed to each other.

It is beyond any effort or precaution of the

master, when he can procure no other labourers, to retrieve the injury he thus sustains. His property is placed at the mercy of his own servants. In the practical operation of the measure, his best and most serviceable people will become the first discontented. They will, as a natural result, be directly induced to suppress their skill, zeal, and willingness to work, or in other ways depreciate their personal value.

When slaves have the power to enforce their freedom from their owners by such a process as that of appraisement, those who are of bad character are comparatively rewarded, while those who are really meritorious are punished.

Thus, on the same estate, a disorderly and unprofitable slave may be readily parted with by his master for fifty pounds, whilst another, a steady, intelligent, and assiduous slave, might, for these good qualities, be worth three hundred. Yet, disproportionate as are the characters and consequent value of the two, the desire for freedom will operate with both ; but how strikingly unequal are the terms upon which they are to obtain the same reward. To the one who is profligate and undeserving the obstacle is trivial. On the contrary, the meritorious slave, applying to his master to know the amount of his ransom, finds it magnified above that of his fellow sixfold. He cannot fail to be struck with the largeness of the amount, and the time requisite to raise it. Such an obvious departure from the principles of common equity, as this, must engender discontent, and prompt the meritorious individual to seek for the cause of this difference in value. He will conceive it gross injustice, that a bad character, who has always disregarded his master's interests, should quickly get his freedom, whilst he himself, who has constantly studied those interests, must wait for it through a course of years lengthened in exact proportion to the value of his services.

When the measure fairly begins to work, the grievance is greatly aggravated.

It is intended, that a proportion of the capital sunk in the lands and buildings of each estate shall be added to the value of each slave.

Earl Bathurst, in his despatch to Sir Benjamin D'Urban, of the 25th February, 1826, says:—

" If, in the process of time, it should be unfor-
" tunately found, that the slaves thus manumitted
" altogether abandon their owners, and refuse to
" work as free persons, the owner not having the
" means, by reason of the Abolition Act, to supply
" the loss of his slaves, and not being able to engage
" any free labourer for his sugar-plantations, the
" price which must then be assigned to the loss
" of each slave must have a direct reference to that
" state in which the plantation will be placed by
" the progressive reduction of the means of culti-
" vating it."

Under this plan it will be the *deserving* slaves who will have to pay for the lands and buildings.

The higher the personal value of the slave, the greater is his *relative* utility to the plantation, and the greater must be the recompense awarded to the proprietor for superseded cultivation. The relative utility of a negro of bad character may thus be estimated at not more than ten pounds, while that of a trustworthy individual may rise so high as one hundred and fifty. In both these cases, the respective sums have to be added to the slave's personal value, before his master can be said to have received an equivalent for his liberation. If the personal value of a slave of bad character be estimated at 50*l.*, the compensation of 10*l.* for his *relative* utility to the plantation being added, will make a sum of 60*l.* only, as the price of his manumission. If the personal value of the skilful and zealous slave be estimated at 300*l.*, the equivalent of 150*l.* for his *relative* utility to the plantation being added, will require as much as 450*l.* to be raised for the purchase of his manumission.

Here the impediment is increased from six to eight fold.

But there is yet further injustice. Not only are different descriptions of cultivation carried on in the colonies, but the same species of cultivation may greatly vary on estates contiguous to each other, from difference of soil, or other local circumstances. Accordingly as those circumstances are more or less favourable, in a corresponding proportion will be the value of the slave, and the appraisers will be called upon to adjust this value, thus varying in different districts of the same colony.

Suppose the fixed capital sunk on a coffee or cotton plantation to be 5,000*l.*, and that sunk on an adjoining sugar plantation to be 25,000*l.*, while each possesses the same number of negroes. One of these from each plantation, of precisely similar capability and character, demands his freedom. The first finds there is to be an addition of but 10*l.* to his price ; not from inferiority of character or skill, but from the accidental circumstance of his living on a plantation where the amount of fixed capital is small. The man from the latter, the sugar estate, finds it, as before stated, so high as 150*l.*, making the difficulty of obtaining freedom perhaps double, as compared with his companion and equal. The same argument would apply even to two estates, which both produced sugar, provided the buildings and machinery on the one were better and more complete than that of the other, or the land more productive.

Thus, the more extensively that machinery has been introduced to facilitate and lighten labour, the more will it be to the prejudice of the slaves. When the supply of labourers is short, to introduce the most advanced and highest description of machinery is all-important and desirable, and the main step to advance a colony to prosperity. But in the new measure proposed, this is checked at once, because no proprietor would think of an outlay, when it could be withdrawn in no other way than by pittances wrung from his best slaves, in their eagerness for freedom.

In contemplating these several facts, can there be a moment's hesitation in regard to the discontent created? Let us imagine a serviceable man on a sugar-plantation applying for his freedom. He has formed in his own mind an estimate of what he ought to pay, and he betakes himself to the appraiser, with the money in his hand. To his astonishment he is asked a sum far beyond his means of payment; he cannot comprehend the cause; and no alternative remains to him but to go back and brood over his disappointment. When he finds his long-cherished hopes utterly frustrated; when, too, he perceives a worthless fellow, distinguished only for idleness and debauchery, now sporting and enjoying himself at liberty all day long, perhaps laughing at the deserving individual who remains in servitude; when he sees his acquaintance on some neighbouring plantation attain his freedom, merely from his chancing to live on an estate where less machinery was used, will he, in common reason, return to his duty a

*

contented man? Is he not goaded on to renounce his better qualities, when he is thus made to feel, that they are insuperable impediments to the attainment of his natural wishes? He discovers that discontent is his surest remedy; that he has only to display the sullenness which he actually feels; that, in one word, he has but to become a bad subject, in order to obtain liberty the more speedily.

Can then the sturdiest champions of compulsory manumission attempt to maintain, that if this man was worth a dollar a day before this occurrence, he will be worth as much still; and if the return from his labour be reduced one-half or two-thirds, will any man contend that a direct violation of property has not been inflicted?

We have confined our attention, hitherto, to the most deserving slaves, because their welfare should be chiefly consulted in every new measure. But with the gang at large the injurious tendency is scarcely less striking. Besides a systematic practice of repressing dexterity and usefulness, the slave may even resort to bodily disablement, in order that his price may be lowered to his means. Such practices are known to exist at present, where there is no higher temptation than that of idling in the sick-house; and there could therefore be little expectation, that the practice would not increase under so much more powerful an inducement. It is vain to argue, that there are reasons, such as the fear of correction from his master or the magistrate, of sufficient weight to deter him from this course —the object for which he strives is perpetually in his view, and will inspire him to brave in its pursuit any present punishment, well knowing that the owner's patience must at length be exhausted.

With the negroes generally, there is also a direct encouragement to theft, since, under the peculiar circumstances of West India cultivation, the master's property is, necessarily, much exposed, and liable to be stolen by his slaves. Even at present, the quantity stolen annually is ascertained to be very great. Crime usually increases in proportion to temptation ; and, under the proposed enactment, the slave must become habituated to fraudulent propensities, and all his ingenuity stimulated to the commission of secret theft. Thus is caused loss of property, both directly and indirectly : directly, by the sum taken from the proprietor in the property stolen ; indirectly, by obstructing the steady government of the plantation, and occasioning unavoidable loss of labour in the services of the slave.

These are vital evils; and can any attempt be made to correct them, particularly the most important one relating to self-depreciation?

Lord Bathurst, in his despatch of the 25th February, 1826, acknowledges, that great mischief would ensue, if manumission were obtained by other means than those of individual and habitual industry; and, in alluding to the possibility of a slave's purchase-money being improperly obtained, his Lordship observes—

" For the sake of the community, indeed, such
" indiscriminate manumissions ought to be prevent-
" ed ; for, undoubtedly, if the purchase-money were
" obtained from any fund which may be formed for
" the liberation of slaves, there would be no test of
" previous habits of industry, of which there is pre-
" sumptive evidence where the money is procured
" by the honest earnings of the slave. To supply
" this defect it may be provided, that in such cases
" a certificate of good conduct for five years should
" be required of the Protector of slaves, before the
" manumission should be completed."

It is not difficult to perceive, that this idea of a certificate is perfectly nugatory. Who is to give it ? The Protector, it seems. How is it possible for the Protector to judge of the private character of the thousands under his charge ? Mr. President Wray, sitting in the Court of Policy, in Demerara, admitted, "that in a population of more than 70,000 " negroes, the protector could not be supposed to be " acquainted with individual characters." To the proposed amendment, that the existence of habits of industry and good conduct should be shown before the same tribunal which inquired into the manner in which the property was obtained, it was urged, that no such tribunal would have better infor-

mation than the protector himself; and any certificate of good behaviour coming from incompetent
judges, must prove altogether futile as regards
protection to the proprietor.

If the framers of the measure had interrogated
managers or overseers as to the length of time
and the close attention it requires to understand
the character of the negroes, even of a mode-
rately-sized gang, they would have little thought
of expecting a single public officer to remedy the
difficulty.

But if the protectors were multiplied from one
to a thousand, and did nothing else but watch over
the individual character of the slaves, the remedy
must be fallacious. On the broad principle of the
measure itself, no system of appraisement, no reference to previous character, can meet the artifices which a slave may employ to depreciate his
value; because many of such artifices, depending
on the suppression of skill or zeal, being of a nega-
tive character, defy detection; and, even were they
detected, detriment to the proprietor's interests
must ensue, since a willing has been changed
into a discontented labourer.

Upon the rising generation, too, of the negroes,
the operation of the same baneful policy of self-
deterioration must increase. The whole of the
youthful class, whose faculties are just dawning,
will be taught to suppress everything like acuteness,

D

and to stifle every indication of future habits of industry.

Compulsory manumission, therefore, contains the worst principle of evil, a principle of growth. Each succeeding year will make more evident to the negroes the means with which they have been invested for self-depreciation ; and each additional instance of its successful adoption by their fellows encourage numbers to resort to the same pernicious artifices.

How miserable, then, is the expedient of *partially* questioning certain individuals in the colonies, who, thus interrogated, may pronounce that in the *present* condition of the slaves the measure would be inoperative, while the same persons, if questioned with a view to the *future* effects of the measure after ten or fifteen years of its adoption, would predict a widely different result !

The writer of the " Remarks" seems unwilling to contemplate the future, and condemns prospective arguments as speculative and merely matter of opinion. But if the negro prefer a state of idleness to one of constrained exertion, it follows that he must earnestly desire to obtain his freedom. If he have repugnance to labour, he will seek his freedom by those means which are easiest. If he possess common reason, he must perceive that the easiest of all methods lies in self-depreciation.

Would it not, then, be contrary to all principles

of equity or sound legislation, to subject what is thus a self-evident proposition to the test of experiment, since, ere the result of that experiment could be ascertained, irreparable injury must have been produced?

In reality, a part only of the subject has been treated of in Lord Bathurst's despatch, and in the " Remarks," inasmuch as they regard only those negroes who may be freed under the operation of the measure, and overlook those who, from inability to procure their freedom, still remain on the plantation.

But it has been shown, that greater deterioration of property may occur from an improper feeling excited among the negroes who remain, than from the more direct loss of labour occasioned by the abstraction of those who become free.

Section 2.

LOSS ARISING, IF A NUMBER OF EFFECTIVE HANDS
BE TAKEN FROM THE PLANTATION.

The capital sunk in land, buildings and machinery is known to be very extensive in West India plantations.

We have now to inquire whether, under the mode proposed, the proprietor will receive fair indemnification for this capital, from the slaves who may obtain their freedom. It is conceived that, in every point of view, loss is occasioned; and that while the plan of increasing the price of the slave according to his relative utility to the estate is calculated to engender the greatest discontent generally, it at the same time affords inadequate compensation to the proprietor, in regard to those who may purchase their manumission.

Lord Bathurst and the writer of the " Remarks" consider the means of fair compensation for the fixed capital to be secured, as appears in the following extract from his Lordship's despatch :—

" If by these regulations an adequate compen-
" sation be not secured to the owner, it must either
" be because the persons who are authorised to
" decide upon the amount are not likely to be fit or
" fair arbitrators, or because there are restrictions
" which will prevent the arbitrators from the free
" exercise of their judgment. Now it must be ad-
" mitted nothing can be fairer than the proposed
" selection of arbitrators in the Trinidad Order: viz.,
" that in the event of the owner and the slave not
" agreeing on the price of the slave's manumission,
" the owner should appoint one, the protector of
" slaves another, and that an umpire should be
" appointed by the chief judge. It is clear that an
" arbitration on such principle would protect the
" interests of the owner, and if there were any ob-
" jection it would be that the bias was in his favour.

" As to restrictions or limitations, there are none to " obstruct the free exercise of their judgment."

To this it may, in the first place, be replied, that the principle of appraisement in its practical operation supposes the price of slaves to continue to be regulated in the West India colonies by competition in the market, like commodities in commerce.

Before we go further, then, let us examine how West India property stands at present.

The following are the Gazette average prices of sugar for the last seven years: viz.,

1820	. .	$35s. \, 0d.$
1821	. .	31 0
1822	. .	29 $4\frac{1}{2}$
1823	. .	34 6
1824	. .	30 $11\frac{1}{2}$
1825	. .	38 $7\frac{1}{4}$
1826	. .	35 $6\frac{1}{2}$

It might be presumed, that the amount of capital which an individual would be willing to vest in the purchase of a property would be proportioned to its net returns. But it can be proved, that in 1819, 65,000*l.* sterling was offered for a sugar-estate in Jamaica, and refused, as below its estimated value. About that period it was considered, that the increasing consumption of sugar, while the means of production were limited, presented a very favourable prospect for the West India planter. Accordingly, in the year 1820, 70,000 *l.* sterling was offered for the abovementioned estate, and also refused for the same reason. But when the proceedings in this country in 1823 and 1824 began to operate, a mighty change took place. It can be shown that distrust gradually arose, and as the proceedings became more and more critical, in the same proportion and as quickly did the value of property progressively decline. The demands of alarmed creditors from all quarters fell on the planters ; they became embarrassed ; and the very same property for which, in 1820, 70,000 *l.* sterling had been refused, when again put up for sale in 1826, found no real bidding higher than 32,000 *l.* currency, being less than 23,000 *l.* sterling.

Strong as this instance appears to be, others equally forcible could be adduced, of the ruinous deterioration of West India property from the like cause ; and they exemplify the nature of those boons which the writer of the " Remarks" affirms to have been accorded to the colonists, and " for which " they should feel grateful."

If a decline in the value of the capital has ensued, whilst the price of the produce has remained nearly the same, it is proof positive that the depreciation of West India property is not attributable to circumstances purely mercantile, but that it is owing to the proceedings of the British legislature.

It is essential to keep this circumstance in mind,

and to examine the mode of appraisement pro-spectively, when the principle of supply and demand no longer exists, as regards the objects to be appraised.

It is apparent, that to allow of a properly-con-stituted market-price, there must be purchasers; but if the principle of compulsory manumission be admitted, after what has been just stated relative to the deterioration in the value of property already produced, will any purchaser of slaves be found? Under the manifold evils detailed in the preceding section, no capitalist henceforward would think of making investments upon West India securities, and all transfer of property would be at an end.

The appraisers are employed to fix a price between conflicting representations of master and slave. But can a criterion for equitable adjust-ment be formed? The slave himself is the only purchaser who appears in the market, and in this condition of things any mode of appraisement must be unjust and injurious to the capitalist which assumes that colonial cultivation will continue un-changed, in the event of the proposed measure being carried into effect; and which does not take into the account the aversion which every capitalist will then feel to making a precarious investment dependent upon the uncertain services of the slaves.

This is founded upon the most simple principle.

If a decrease in the value of capital have already occurred beyond what is attributable to circumstances purely mercantile, and is solely occasioned by the threatened measures of Government, it is a fair inference that a further decrease would ensue if such threatened measures were put into execution; and the effects of that opinion prevailing throughout the colonies, must render the chance of fully withdrawing the fixed capital more and more precarious, as the evils of the measure became more widely developed.

Let us suppose a sugar-plantation, with two hundred negroes, worth 40,000 *l.* ; one-half sunk in lands and buildings, the other half the value of the slaves. Accordingly as the negroes progressively free themselves, the 20,000 *l.* sunk in lands and buildings has to be apportioned among them, and added to the price of their manumission. Now it must be recollected, that *the whole* of the two hundred negroes are requisite to carry on profitable cultivation. The land and buildings cannot be disposed of, or circumscribed to suit a more limited business, as would be the case with premises in this country when a manufacturer reduced the number of his workmen.

After a number of men, then, are freed, the proprietor is left with a great concern upon his hands without people to carry it on. To be fully remunerated for the property sunk in that concern, the people remaining would have to pay, as he gradually becomes more and more short of hands, a prodigious sum for their freedom. Is it possible, from what has been stated, that he could receive full indemnification? Let it be recollected, that it will soon be, not a quota, but the *entire* of the fixed capital, which the efficient negroes, applying for freedom, will have to pay to indemnify their masters,—and in actual practice can this be done?

The writer of the " Remarks" illustrates the case by comparing a sugar-estate to a mill with a number of buckets! The reader, it is presumed, will be tempted to smile at the idea of considering the negroes as mere passive machines, devoid of those feelings, passions, and intelligence, which it is their master's chief solicitude to call into existence.

But, to pass over the narrow and partial view of the subject here displayed, even were we to indulge the writer in his singular mode of illustration, it fails to establish his object. He says, if twenty buckets are attached to a wheel, and four be removed, the proprietor will be entitled to be remunerated for whatever loss of work this removal occasioned; and if the work turned off were diminished, from incompetency of power in the wheel, not only in the proportion of twenty to sixteen, being one-fifth, but in the proportion of two-fifths, then would the proprietor be entitled to receive, as equitable compensation, two-fifths of the value in place of one.

Now it is important to reflect, that if four buckets be taken away from the wheel, its motion may not only be diminished in a greater ratio than two-fifths, but it may be *stopped altogether*.

This is the proper application of such an illustration to the circumstances of a sugar-estate. If forty efficient negroes be removed out of two hundred, being the same proportion as in the assumed case of the buckets, will any person, acquainted with the colonies, maintain that cultivation could continue? An estate which had produced two hundred hogsheads of sugar would not merely be reduced two-fifths of that amount, that is to say, to one hundred and twenty hogsheads, but it would be altogether abandoned, because its returns would not cover its expenses.

The author of the bucket-illustration must be sensible of its fallacy, if he reflect that at some one point, the wheel, from its diminution of buckets, must stop.

The question is, as regards the cultivation of sugar, will this point soon be reached? Little is required to be said on this head, if the proprietors are prepared to establish the fact, that even at present they can scarcely spare one man.

Lord Bathurst acknowledges, indeed, the ultimate

improbability that the slaves could of themselves indemnify their master for the entire capital he has sunk; and his Lordship says, when the price of manumission rises from 100 to 500*l.*, then it will be time for the nation to come forward. A most consolatory prospect! And what are the proprietors to do *before the nation does come forward?* When the discussion is beginning, and before the public are disposed to put their hands into their pockets, the proprietor's buildings, machinery, roads, dams, are going into dilapidation, and he is a ruined man.

When we prove injury in the principle, it is scarcely necessary to descend to discuss the practice. Many colonists view with alarm the great power given to the Protector, and other officers of government. But let us pass over details. It is only necessary to reflect upon what the appraiser has to do, to perceive that the mode of working must be as bad as the design, and that the whole process must be vague and mere guess-work. Even admitting the very doubtful proposition, that impartial arbitrators could be selected, numerous peculiarities may exist to obstruct the formation of a sound judgment in regard to the value of a part of the planter's stock, in consequence of the manner in which the whole is rendered profitable.

It is to repeat the opinion of every intelligent person recently returned from the colonies, to declare, that it is perfectly impossible for any appraiser, no matter how intelligent, experienced, or impartial, correctly to estimate the value of a slave, in order to award compensation in the manner described by Lord Bathurst.

Section 3.

PLANTATIONS BURDENED WITH EXPENSES, WHILE THE GROSS RETURNS ARE DIMINISHED.

Having shown, in the preceding section, that the fixed capital of an estate cannot be removed, we have now to show that the necessary expenses of carrying on its cultivation cannot be diminished.

Each proprietor is by law obliged to maintain the aged, the infirm, and the helpless, upon his estate. This duty he performs with the utmost cheerfulness. He can hold out to his able negroes no stronger incentive to good conduct than the assurance verified in their parents, that they will pass the evening of life in rest and contentment, with every little want provided for. The spectacle itself is one of the most agreeable which can strike the eye of the stranger; it is peculiarly grateful to the feelings of the negro; and most forcibly illustrates the happy state of things when benefits are made to flow from the master alone. Compulsory manumission severs the link which makes this obligation mutual, for it gives to the master all the expense, and deprives him of the benefit.

On most West India plantations not more than one-third part of each gang can be considered as efficient for field-cultivation, there being included the old and infirm, the infant and the helpless, all of whom are unserviceable, but whom the proprietor is bound by every consideration to support.

The young and able, those in the prime of life, and under the strongest influence of the passions, to whom all the allurements of idleness present themselves in full force, would lose no time in availing themselves of any opportunity to go at large.

On the contrary, the old slaves on a plantation, in whom the ardent passions have subsided, knowing that they must soon come to be exempt from work, and entitled to that maintenance gratuitously from their master, which in a state of freedom they would have to earn for themselves, would make no attempt to procure their own liberation, but would devote their earnings, and any accumulation of money they may have already made, to the ransom of their children.

This double operation, therefore, of the young and efficient freeing themselves, or being freed by their aged connexions; and the superannuated and infirm remaining to be supported by the proprietor, would leave the burdens of a plantation undiminished, while its ability to bear them was nearly annihilated.

With regard to the other portion, from whom no labour is obtained, namely, the infants, the proprietor is induced at present to treat them with the utmost care, were it only for their future value. But the prospect of obtaining their future services might soon be changed.

Slavery, considered as an hereditary condition, is perpetuated on the side of the mother only; if means were taken to purchase all the female children, no calculation regarding relative value could be made, and the property of each proprietor must become extinct with the lives of his present negroes.

Now it is fair to apprehend, that the means of obtaining manumission might be improperly employed, for the purpose of exterminating slavery, regardless of all injury to the capitalist. Whether those means would be supplied from a fund raised in this country by speculative theorists hostile to the colonies, or, whether the slaves themselves would be, by such persons, instigated to purchase the female children, the result would be equally injurious to the proprietor.

Section 4.

CONTRARY TO THE LAW OF MORTGAGE.

Few persons require to be told, that the proportion of property under mortgage in the West Indies is considerable. It is singular, that, in the various discussions to which the Colonial Question has given rise, so little attention has been directed to the interests thus involved. Independently of the mortgagees themselves, it is the direct advantage of the planters to have every facility open for the raising of loans to meet temporary difficulties.

The act of Parliament, the 13 Geo. III. c. 14, invites loans from aliens, on the security of leasehold or freehold estates, in His Majesty's West Indian Colonies. The 14 Geo. III. c. 79 legalizes the taking of interest by British subjects, for sums advanced on mortgage, and securities of any lands, tenements, hereditaments, slaves, and other things, at the rate allowed by the law of the colony where the mortgaged property lies. And the 3 Geo. IV. c. 47, further regulates the rate of interest, and extends its provisions to persons advancing capital in this country.

On the faith of these enactments, large investments on mortgage have been made. Slaves are recognised in them, as property in fee-simple, absolute, which has been confirmed by decisions in our courts, both of law and equity. Consequently, all mortgagees rest their security not on Colonial enactments, but on British Acts of Parliament; and the law relating to mortgaged property in the colonies must be analogous to the law relating to mortgaged property in England.

By the law of England, when woods or messuages are included in a mortgage, none of those woods or messuages can be sold or alienated, either collectively or in part, by the mortgagor, or by any other known authority, even though the proceeds of such sale should be appropriated to the benefit of the mortgagee, without the express consent and concurrence of the latter; the law giving to him the sole privilege of determining as to whatever may affect his security

By the same law of England, when slaves are expressly specified in a mortgage on West India property, neither the proprietor, nor any other known authority, can legally sell such slaves, even though the proceeds be applied in liquidation of the mortgage, unless it be with the previous consent of the mortgagee.

Yet it does not appear, that Earl Bathurst has explicitly provided for the claims of the mortgagee, who has lent his money in the firm reliance that the law has guaranteed, both to himself and to the mortgagor, the full effects of the stipulation of the mortgage contract.

But if the slaves, being in law real property, on which the mortgagee holds a.lien, be permitted at their will to separate themselves from the plantation, it must weaken the security of the mortgagee, by removing the instruments through which the fixed capital was rendered productive, and by the employment of which for the benefit of the mortgagor, there was a reasonable confidence that the mortgage might ultimately be redeemed.

And in regard to the purchase-money paid by the slave to his owner, as the price of his liberation, if the amount go at once into the hands of the mortgagee, it is an injustice to the debtor, because he had a right to expect a rate of profit from his cultivation, much higher than the mere interest paid for his loan ; and it is illegal, because it is beyond the terms of his contract with the mortgagee.

If, again, the money be deposited in some public chest, it is illegal and unjust to both parties: unjust, because the removal of an efficient hand entered not into the calculations of the owner of the plantation, and by the decrease of its produce from subtracted labour, he finds his debt not diminishing but growing larger, while the mortgagee runs the risk of losing his money;—illegal, because the stipulation forms no part of the mortgage contract.

E

When we show that illegality is added to injustice, we may close the case on the part of the proprietor.

Let us sum up the objections.

If not one man is freed, compulsory manumission changes his good slaves into bad ones. If any are freed, he gets inadequate remuneration for their loss. It unjustly makes the burdens on his estates perpetual; and in case of mortgages, is contrary to the statute-law of the realm.

Is compulsory manumission then compatible with a fair and equitable consideration of the rights of private property? Will any member of the legislature be willing to confirm an act of the executive, which is expressly contrary to the Resolution to which Parliament became pledged in 1823?

Chapter IV.

INJURY TO THE WELL-BEING OF THE SLAVES.

It is presumed, that the great object contemplated by the British nation is to civilize the blacks living in our colonies. The crime of taking them from their own country is long past by; but it surely cannot be intended to compensate them for their former wrongs, by replunging them into barbarism. Yet it is to be feared that this is the consummation to result from compulsory manumission.

Section 1.

COUNTERACTS THE INCENTIVES TO CIVILISATION.

A free peasantry in the colonies is the desideratum sought by the framers of the measure. It is argued, that men are creatures of habit, and that if the negro, by voluntary industry, amass such a sum as will procure his ransom, the habit of working will have become firmly established, and he will continue to labour when he has obtained his freedom.

This argument has been entirely refuted by the simple question, What is the *motive* for exertion in the two cases? Before the negro became free, he had the strongest of inducements perpetually present to his mind—the attainment of freedom, or the privilege of enjoying himself uncontrolled. It was not for the money that he worked, but for that which the money would procure him. When he has, at length, attained his freedom, what motive has he to work further? Name one object, equivalent, in his estimation, to the irksomeness of labour; the one-inspiring aim is attained, the stimulus is gone.

But it is not enough for our purpose to show, that industry is eventually superseded. We can establish, that the very means held out are themselves the most efficacious in producing this pernicious result. It is said that men are creatures of habits, and do not speedily change them. We meet our opponents on this ground.

If you demand of a man, living in a country imperfectly civilised, for what reason he works, he will answer, that he may purchase food. But put the same question to a man in a state highly civilised, and he will reply, that besides the purchase of food, he requires good clothing, lodging, and other comforts which have become *habitual* to him, and in which custom would make it disreputable in him not to indulge.

Let us apply this to the negro in the West Indies. At present his artificial wants are extremely low; and if certain habits, such as above described, have to operate hereafter upon him as incentives to exertion, is it not requisite that they should now begin to be established? Suppose a negro, by rearing stock of various descriptions, can earn a dollar per week—should he not be taught to lay out that sum in the purchase of articles, for instance, of personal decoration for himself and family, or of additional conveniences in his hut, in the display of which he will henceforth take a pride?

By such means it must be, that, in the lapse of time, he will feel that he must work longer than is merely necessary to procure him food, because he has other wants to satisfy.

But compulsory manumission directly counteracts this process. It prompts him to the most sordid self-denial. Its language to him is—" Spend not your weekly dollar, but rather hoard it with the most scrupulous rigour; improve not the condition of your family:—in a word, confine your wants to the state of the savage."

The necessary consequence will be, that when he attains to freedom, all his physical wants remain unchanged. And are these the boasted steps which have been taken to elevate the condition of the slaves? It is certainly a novel mode of establishing a free peasantry, to commence by divesting them of every stimulus to exertion.

Section 2.

DEBAUCHERY AND CRIME ENCOURAGED.

It will not have escaped the observation of the intelligent reader, that if compulsory manumission leads to self-depreciation, by directly suggesting and encouraging a suppression of dexterity and usefulness, the same end may be attained by debasing the moral character. Every species of debauchery is, in point of fact, encouraged, to constrain the proprietor to offer little impediment to the freedom of his slaves.

Good conduct frequently renders a negro more valuable even than skill, and it thus becomes a principal impediment to the attainment of his freedom. In the case of a drunken, worthless character on a plantation, the proprietor, instead of opposing his liberation, will be glad to get rid of him at a small amount, because he is continually giving trouble and setting a bad example.

If there be any truth in the maxim of moralists, that the road to vice is alluring in itself, what must be the result when men are urged upon it, by the strongest incentives which can be supposed to operate with them? The profligate slave may purchase his freedom within a year,—the virtuous has to wait for it ten years, and perhaps all his life, without success. What is this but to teach him, in the most emphatic manner, that if he were but profligate and worthless, he would find no such difficulties? Under the common operations of human nature, it is impossible, when the whole moral code is reversed—when virtue is punished and vice rewarded, that any number of men in a state like that of the negroes will continue virtuous.

We shall here be again reminded about the certificate of good character which is to be required. But if this question be to be discussed at all by men of business, it is surely time to dismiss this alleged safeguard of a certificate. It can never, as we have shown, be of the least avail in reference to skill; and as a real preventive it must equally prove nugatory in regard to moral conduct. Without intending any disrespect, it must be pronounced to savour a little of the ludicrous.

Let us suppose some measure introduced into one of the counties of England, affecting its population as vitally as compulsory manumission affects the slaves in our colonies, and what would be thought of any person who should gravely propose, that a public officer, amid other multifarious duties, should certify minutely as to the individual character of every man in the county? If we were to circumscribe his jurisdiction to a few square miles, or even to a few streets of one town, the thing must plainly be impossible.

Dissimulation, hypocrisy, and craft, are often described as the parents of crime, and they will be inevitably resorted to, to screen the vices of the slave. His maxim will be, Let me become a vicious subject, to lower my value with my master, and let me become an adept in cunning to deceive the protector.

The higher his intellectual attainments, the easier will it be for him to practise this deception with success; and while, as has been shown in the preceding section, the beneficial attributes of future civilisation are checked, the slave is habituated to its corruptions.

None of the palliators of the measure can get over this conclusion, that if flagrant crime be not openly encouraged, it cannot be denied that it is fostered secretly. How many will be the plans laid for stealing in the dark; and for this evil there is no cure. If the delinquent be detected, it depreciates his character, and, consequently, his value; and, if undiscovered, it swells the fund which is to make him free.

Section 3.

VIRTUOUS UNION OF THE SEXES IMPEDED.

If we wish to infuse a higher sense of moral feeling among the slaves, it is indispensable to elevate their ideas in regard to the virtuous union of the sexes. There is no one of the measures of amelioration which has attracted more attention, or which is more desired by the British community.

We often hear that there is too great a temptation to immorality in this particular among the colonists. It may undoubtedly be true; but still illicit connexions are materially checked by the dread of bringing into existence an offspring whose lot by birth would be slavery.

If compulsory manumission be enforced, this

salutary barrier is removed, because the freedom of any female slave could be purchased by the person desirous of cohabiting with her, and her offspring would be free. Thus, on the parties colluding to take advantage of the new measure, the greatest mischiefs would accrue to the community.

If this practice once obtained, and were found easy of accomplishment, the female slaves would have a powerful inducement to court illicit connexion with the whites, in preference to marriage with men of their own condition. One of the chief objects of amelioration would thus be frustrated, and the offspring of these connexions become liable to be left destitute in case of the sickness, absence, or death of the father, and consequently thrown upon the casual charity of the public.

Besides the immorality thus in the first instance produced, how fruitful a source of future crime is presented!

Section 4.

TASK-WORK PREVENTED.

When we examine the measure as it will more immediately affect the domestic government of each plantation, we find objections equally forcible with those already stated.

In none of Mr. Canning's orations on the subject has he been so eloquent as when he described the effect of abolishing impending coercion, upon the feelings of the slave. He depicted in the most powerful manner the beautiful effects that would ensue when the slave performed his work with alacrity, and his condition assimilated to that of the voluntary labourer. It was here that he expatiated upon the wisdom of allowing benefits to the slave to flow from the master, since it would incite them to work without the necessity for coercion. The system of task-work would be introduced, which perhaps is the greatest practical improvement in the condition of slavery.

It is quite evident that this system can only exist with the agreement and reciprocal feeling of both parties. The slave knows well that his master can return to the old system at his will, and this reflection is the chief cause for establishing the improvement. The master knows well, that the law empowers him to keep his slaves at work till six in the evening; but he considers that, if he can elicit their spontaneous skill and assiduity, they will get through an equal quantity of work by an earlier hour, and will pursue their labour cheerfully. He is therefore disposed to approve of task-work wherever it is practicable, both under the influence of that more humane spirit which pervades the colonies, and from the desire to save himself the trouble and expense of superintendence in the field.

Under this beneficial regulation, the negroes are

found to complete their day's work by as early an hour as three or four o'clock, having then the remainder of the day at their own disposal, to earn money for themselves. The master never thinks of objecting to such earnings, which benefit his people without injuring himself. On the contrary, it is to his advantage, by increasing their contentment, the salutary operation of which we have described in a preceding section.

But let compulsory manumission be insisted on, and how differently will he then contemplate the earnings of his slaves! At present their little funds are spent in harmless amusements—in adorning their persons, and giving Christmas and other holiday entertainments, in which it is their delight to mimic the manners of the whites. But change the scene, and let them employ their earnings to procure their freedom, and what will be the master's course? He will be constrained, in self-defence to stop their means of earning. He will discontinue task-work, and keep his negroes working until six o'clock, as the law allows him.

Let us banish Utopian views from our thoughts, and consider, as practical men, is it ever to be expected—is it reasonable, that colonial proprietors would act otherwise? You drive them to it. They have vested their property on the express declaration of the law, that they are entitled to the labour of their slaves until *six o'clock*. You cannot change this hour for an earlier one, without infringing the rights of property, in a manner which could never possibly be contemplated by any legislature. There is therefore no regulation which can obviate the evil. Task-work, consisting of a multiplicity of details, cannot in its very nature be commanded or enforced by any other authority than that of the master. Its beneficial effects upon the slaves consist in the master's entering into their feelings, and giving them encouragement precisely in the degree that personal trouble in management is removed.

When property in slaves is made but a precarious interest, dependent upon the slaves themselves, it is no more than the truth to assert, that a rigorous system of coercion, such as prevailed in the colonies some twenty years ago, would return.

If it be argued, that this involves a contradiction in reference to the *contentment*, described as being the proprietor's chief object to establish, let it be recollected that he is now in a dilemma. If he allows his slaves to accumulate earnings, they may be employed to his own *total ruin ;* he has therefore to get, as speedily as possible, the utmost degree of work from his labourers that the law allows him.

Section 5.

INVIDIOUS FEELINGS EXCITED BY PROMPTING TO A GENERAL RUSH FOR FREEDOM.

Several of His Majesty's ministers, in various declarations and speeches, have alluded to the institution of slavery in ancient times ; and availing themselves of the great experience thus presented for guidance and direction, have affirmed that the same measures of amelioration should be introduced to mitigate slavery in the West India colonies, which had in times past mitigated slavery in Europe. By obvious analogy, if the experience of times past be the true guide in measures relating to amelioration, the same experience should be the guide for measures relating to emancipation.

Let us examine, then, if this be the case.

In all ages and records of history, and in every nation on the globe in which slavery has existed, the difficulties of manumission have become less and less as civilisation advanced. But by the mode of operation laid down by Lord Bathurst, the difficulties in the present case must gradually increase. In a gang of one hundred negroes, the first man applying for freedom would have his relative utility to the plantation estimated at a small sum, the loss of the services of an individual not materially impeding its cultivation. But if thirty or forty men were to be abstracted from the estate, the sum to be assessed as relative utility must rise in a rapidly increased ratio, the remaining hands being wholly incompetent to render the fixed capital productive.

Supposing, then, the measure to possess an executory principle: in the first year, according to its projectors, a man might procure his freedom at 100*l.* At the end of the second year, a man of precisely the same capabilities and abstract value would find the price of manumission risen to 150*l.* At the end of the third year it might rise to 200*l.*; and so on, progressively, until it mounted to 500*l.*, or a still higher sum.

This is the operation consequent on the terms employed by Earl Bathurst, and subsequently, indeed, explicitly avowed by him, to illustrate the measure.

It has been considered, and repeatedly declared by His Majesty's ministers, that a progressive amelioration in the condition of the slaves, the diffusion of moral instruction, the just appreciation of the blessings of a pure religion, and a gradual reformation in manners and opinions, should continue to exercise their salutary influence, until slavery insensibly glided into freedom.

Yet compulsory manumission proceeds in express contradiction to this principle. It teaches the slave, that the sooner he demands his freedom the easier it will be for him to succeed. It discourages the idea of delaying till the morals be improved by instruction, and it urges him to rush forward at once by the most expeditious course, by teaching him, that those only who delay incur the danger of disappointment.

The public at large have been harangued about the *gradual operation* of the measure. What will be their surprise when they understand, that the meaning of such gradual operation simply is, that the difficulties in attaining the object sought should become greater by degrees instead of less? It is, indeed, a notable specimen of legislation, to announce to theslaves,—Now that you are ignorant, you may procure your freedom for 100*l.* ; but some years hence, when you have improved by instruction, you will have to pay five times as much.

Under such excitements, a measure which works on the predominant passions of men, awakening in them mutual feelings of envy and distrust, prompting each to take advantage of his fellow, and universally forestalling the fruits of civilisation, must be utterly incompatible with the well-being of the slave.

Who, therefore, can maintain, all the circumstances enumerated in the foregoing sections taken in conjunction, that compulsory manumission is in conformity with the Resolution of Parliament?

Chapter V.

SAFETY OF THE COLONIES ENDANGERED.

The correspondence of Mr. Canning with Mr. Galatin, lately published, evinces plainly the importance which is attached to our transatlantic possessions. It cannot be supposed that a minister of state will hold one tone to a foreign power, and a different one to ourselves.

It is on occasions of public diplomacy, when our own policy is opposed to that of the great rising republic of America, that the full swell of public opinion makes known the extent of interest felt by the British nation towards her colonies.

The love of dominion is natural to mankind, and few like to lose what they have once possessed ; but, with the reflecting part of the nation, this feeling is strengthened by the consciousness that slavery itself will be promoted by the destruction of the British colonies. Foreign nations will take up what we abandon ; and if we are still to consume sugar, the state of the continental markets proves to a demonstration that that consumption will be supplied by slave-labour, and not by free labour from either east or west.

Hence the safety of the colonies not only affects

the dignity of His Majesty's crown, which ministers have sworn to uphold; but it combines every consideration on this question which can influence the conduct of an independent member of the legislature.

If, then, there ever was a measure which involved a dilemma, it is that of compulsory manumission. It must either be operative, or, from the restrictions with which it is fenced, it must be inoperative.

Let us view it in both ways.

Section 1.

CULTIVATION SUPERSEDED.

It is almost unnecessary to remark, that the nature of the colonial system assumes the production in the colonies of commodities possessing exchangeable value, to be transported to the mother-country for sale, and tending, in the various relations of their transport, to promote and invigorate the national commerce.

But if the negroes free themselves in the manner proposed, this commerce must cease.

The writer of the " Remarks" has made one acknowledgment which greatly abridges the necessity for argument or examination on this head. He says, that no instance has yet occurred of free negroes working steadily for hire in the field, in the British

F

colonies; and that it is not to be expected that they will so work, until their physical wants have been augmented.

Now it has been shown, in the first section of the preceding chapter, that those wants, instead of being augmented, or even established, are effectually checked by the new measure. If there could be, in the first instance, a hope that cultivation might hereafter be conducted by free labourers, it is destroyed in its bud; and precisely in the degree that the negroes are freed, will the value of the colonies decline.

Political economy is now the fashion. All who are connected with the Legislature, or who take a part in public affairs, are anxious to display their proficiency in this science. Without further comment, an appeal is made to them to pronounce, on weighing well the reasoning referred to, if profitable cultivation in the colonies will not be superseded.

What, then, would be the object of protecting those colonies? They would virtually be lost to this country, in express contradiction to the declared policy of the Legislature.

Section 2.

REBELLION INSTIGATED.

On the other hand, let us suppose compulsory manumission inoperative; that Government discover its latent difficulties, and that they wish ostensibly to enforce its enactment while they fetter it with restrictions to prevent its practical working.

Here it is conceived that still more disastrous consequences would ensue. You tell the negro that he has a right to purchase his freedom ; and when he comes forward to claim it, he finds himself mocked and imposed upon.

In common reason, is this the kind of legislation we are to expect after the many warnings we have had of negro susceptibility, and the well-grounded conviction that there are embers, only wanting one kindling breath to involve the whole colonies in destruction?

Since the agitation of negro emancipation, within these few years past, a great excitement has prevailed among the slaves, and mischief on no common scale has occurred, merely from the delusion practised upon the negroes as to the pretended benefits intended them. During the insurrection in Demerara, when the insurgents were told by the governor, of the new laws and indulgences to be granted them, they received the boon with comparative derision ; they said, to quote the words of the Governor's despatch, that " those things were " no comforts for them ; that they were tired of " being slaves ; that their good King had sent orders " that they should be free, and that they would not " work any more."

By obvious analogy we may judge of the danger
if an inoperative law be now passed. To inspire
hopes which can never be realized, is at any time
bad; but in the case of the slaves, it is to render
them for ever dissatisfied with their lot, and to
arouse every angry passion in their minds. The
strongest indignation, therefore, should be expressed
at attempts made to palliate the manifold errors of
the measure, or to procure the unreflecting concurrence of parties locally interested, by represent-
ing that it might ostensibly be allowed to pass, if
rendered inoperative, because then no harm can
result from it. Such a mode of proceeding to all
parties concerned, both master and slave, would be
unworthy of the British Government, and not more
disingenuous than impolitic.

Imagine, for a moment, the feelings of a slave,
who, relying upon the efficacy of the law promulgated, applies for his freedom, but finds all a
fallacy! Think of his baffled hope—the pinings
of the heart—the burning sense of injustice! And
it is all-important to reflect, that the obnoxious
object of these excited passions will be the master,
or the resident proprietor. The negro will never
believe that he has been deceived by the King of
England. He will decide, that the King has con-
ferred on him the boon, and that it has been inter-
cepted by combination of the colonial proprietors.

The negroes are just beginning to be sensible
that amelioration is different from what they first

imagined it. Proclamations and proceedings of the governors have tended to check their fatal impression that a life of idleness was now at hand; but if you disturb the existing tranquillity, if you again raise the delusive cry of " Freedom!" may we not apprehend that kindred spirits, brooding over their fancied wrongs, will coalesce, and discontent thus swell into rebellion. It is vain to disguise or cloak the measure. Every colonial proprietor knows the excitement that will always be kept up by the anti-colonial party. " If I am to be robbed," he will say, " rather let me suffer at once, than be kept in perpetual dread of ruin. If a slave worth 300 *l.* comes to demand his freedom, better suffer a loss of 100 *l.* than send him back with a refusal, for assuredly he will never be a peaceable or good subject again." In his own defence, therefore, he must refuse to sanction any modifications of a measure which will equally injure himself, and endanger the public safety.

Whether, then, compulsory manumission contain an executory principle, or otherwise, it is incompatible with the safety of the colonies.

We have now contemplated the measure in every point of view, and it must be emphatically pronounced to be contrary both to the letter and the spirit of the Resolutions of both houses of Parliament.

Chapter VI.

NO JUST ANALOGY IN THE PRECEDENTS AD-
DUCED BY GOVERNMENT.

A thousand precedents would never justify a bad measure—it may therefore be deemed superfluous to offer a remark on this head; but as Mr. Canning has argued, that whatever is adopted in one colony can safely be introduced into all the rest, and as this maxim has been taken for granted by many persons willing to save themselves the trouble of thinking, it is necessary to enter into some explanation.

Section 1.

TRINIDAD.

When the order in council for negro treatment was sent out to Trinidad, great objections were offered, both generally, and to the individual clauses which constitute compulsory manumission.

It is not necessary here to inquire how often that order has been altered, or the reasons why the colonists of Trinidad have been constrained to submit to the authority imposed upon them. We have only to show that the case of that island differs from that of the other British colonies.

Trinidad was originally a Spanish colony; its laws were framed previously to the abolition of the slave-trade, and have continued unaltered since the cession of the island to Great Britain.

Now it is apparent that, when fresh slaves can be procured, compulsory manumission is not so objectionable; because the place of those who purchase their freedom can be immediately filled up by others.

It has consequently been considered that, while the slave-trade was in active operation in the Spanish colonies, the practice of manumission was encouraged, as increasing the means of preventing insurrection.

But it is surely unfair to hold up to the imitation of another colony the enactments and usages introduced by one whose laws were adapted to a state of things so different; and to require that the provisions of a code adapted to the existence of the slave-trade, should be engrafted upon other codes framed since its abolition.

The order in council for Trinidad has not affected the principle of the Spanish law, or rather the practice in the Spanish colonies, which allows a slave to enfranchise himself by purchase. But the British law in our settlements gives no such right whatever to a slave.

According to those codes, the interest of an owner in his slave is that of a fee-simple absolute:

he purchased upon that tenure, he has continued to hold upon the same, and cannot be deprived of that legal title without a direct violation of property.

In Trinidad it is otherwise: a person purchasing a slave in that colony, knows beforehand that he acquires only a precarious title in such a slave, which depends on the ability of the slave to purchase himself.

Nor has sufficient time yet elapsed to make known the great difference in the working of the measure that must take place now that the slave-trade has ceased, contrasted with the period when it was in active prosecution.

It ought also to be stated, that the hardship and evils of the law in Trinidad, even subsequent to the abolition of the slave-trade, had not been so much felt, from the nature of its laws not being generally known in this country: consequently, there was no extraneous excitement upon the subject given to the minds of the negroes.

But now, when this excitement has been given, the brief experience already afforded, tends strongly to corroborate the arguments we have advanced; and it is credibly asserted, that the Secretary for the Colonies has received representations and appeals, proving evils to have proceeded from the operation of this law.

Among these evils, theft is shown to have increased; and the proceedings before the local magistrates are said to evince a progressive demo‑ralization amongst the negroes.

It is further known, that instances have occurred where the sum assessed by the appraisers, as the price of manumission, has been higher than the negro was able, or considered himself entitled, to pay ; and the being sent back under these circumstances has visibly produced in him a sullenness and discontent exactly as has been described, and in all probability as injurious to the interests of his master, as if he had obtained his discharge at his own valuation.

From these circumstances, it is apparent that there is no analogy between the case of Trinidad and that of the other British Colonies, and that thus far no proper precedent is established.

Section 2.

ST. LUCIE.

In regard to this colony, the measure has been but recently introduced, and without the spontaneous concurrence of its inhabitants. It was established there by the force of arbitrary authority There was no adequate court or power, similar in constitution and functions to the Assemblies in the other islands, to resist its promulgation ; and the threat conveyed in the despatch of Earl Bathurst to the

Governor, thus amounted to an imperative mandate for the adoption of the measure as law in the colony. Is this a precedent?

Section 3.

BERBICE.

The case of Berbice is still more flagrant. This colony possessed, a short time back, a council composed of persons having property at stake. Before the enactments relating to the slaves in that colony were brought forward, this council was dismissed, and another arbitrarily appointed, consisting of persons having no interest in the cultivation of the colony.

It was previously declared, that the new laws relating to the slaves, in whatever way they might be finally settled, should not be carried into operation at Berbice, unless the same measures were at the same time adopted in Demerara. In the latter colony, all the measures relating to amelioration were received, and compulsory manumission alone rejected; but in Berbice, the new council, so appointed and so composed, passed the latter measure contrary to the wish of every proprietor in the colony.

It ought moreover to be stated that, before the new laws were promulgated in Demerara, they were sent home to Lord Bathurst for confirma-

tion, upon which his Lordship observes,—" The
" King has been graciously pleased to approve
" the decision that you adopted, of referring the
" draft of the Act to his Majesty, for his considera-
" tion, instead of immediately promulgating it as a
" law in the colony."

But how does the new Council of Berbice act?
The most important of all the new measures they
carry at once into effect; that is to say, they allow
no opportunity for parties in England to carry
remonstrance or explanation to the foot of the
throne.

Again, let us ask, is this a precedent? What is
the meaning of the term? does it not warrant the
inference, in this case, that some assembly, .com-
posed of parties interested, have given their concurrence? But how marked is the difference
between a council composed of persons possessing
little or no property in slaves, and a court where
several of the members hold large plantations, and
are deeply interested in the permanent prosperity
of their colony.

The possession of this large stake by the members, and the circumstance of having delegated
interests to represent, peculiarly conduce to safe
and practicable legislation. Such circumstances
present a security against precipitancy,—prompt
to a careful and minute consideration of all local
peculiarities,—and procure for every public measure a full and patient examination of all its rela-

tions, both direct and contingent, before it is permitted to be put in execution.

And further, in respect to any one of these West-India cases, has there elapsed a time sufficient to enable us to estimate the policy of the experiment, and still less to pronounce upon its fitness for the whole of our West-Indian possessions?

Section 4.

CAPE OF GOOD HOPE.

How this colony should be referred to as a precedent it is difficult to explain. Its climate differs materially from that of the West Indies. In the latter, the evils apprehended from giving freedom to the slaves arise from the impossibility of procuring free labourers to supply their place. It is but a very short time since emigration from this country to the Cape of Good Hope was greatly encouraged; and it is ascertained, by experience, that Europeans can work without injury or inconvenience in that climate.

Thus the supply of voluntary labourers not only existing, but increasing in that colony, the inducements to perpetuate slavery must progressively expire, and slaves may consequently be freed without injury to the property of their owners, or danger to the public safety.

From this obvious difference in physical circumstances between the West India colonies and the

Cape of Good Hope, there is no just analogy between the two; and though compulsory manumission may be enacted in the one, it cannot, therefore, be taken as a model for imitation to the other.

This straining after inapplicable precedent clearly indicates deficiency of argument.

No enactment containing inherently a principle of evil, even though acceded to willingly, or acquiesced in passively, by individual bodies, should ever be set up by a wise government as an example for general adoption.

It has been more than once remarked in Parliament, by persons of high character, that the precedent generally existing throughout the Spanish colonies served as a sufficient ground for the measure.

But there are two points which should never be omitted in reflecting on the question :

I. As to the opportunity of procuring other labourers.

II. The difference of amount sunk in fixed capital, between the Spanish colonies and those of Great Britain.

In regard to the first, fresh labourers can be procured in the Spanish colonies, but cannot in the British; and in regard to the second, there must surely be some difference in the working of a measure when the amount of capital to be withdrawn varies in the proportion of 20,000*l.* in the one case, to a few hundreds in the other.

Chapter VII.

RESPONSIBILITY ATTACHING TO MINISTERS IF THEY ENFORCE COMPULSORY MANUMISSION.

Whoever notices the levity of manner with which this question is treated, would imagine that our constitution had undergone a change, and that His Majesty's advisers were relieved from responsibility for the acts of the executive. On any occasion it is a rash step to counsel the crown to important measures before a full investigation has been instituted. But when a step is taken so contrary to the laws of the realm, as, by eminent law-authorities, Compulsory Manumission, in regard to mortgaged property, is conceived to be, *responsibility* ceases to be an idle term, and circumstances may arise from it to disturb the peace of a minister of state much longer than he anticipates.

It can never be too often repeated that, so far as legislation for the negroes is concerned, what is once done is irrevocable. In other public measures, an opportunity is afforded to a minister, when he makes a false step, to change his policy by a dexterous manœuvre. But no such resource being afforded in the West India Question, we should conclude that more cautious deliberation would in the first instance be exercised, and that a *full examination* would take place before excitement was created by announcing even the heads of a new measure. The proceedings hitherto have been on a principle directly opposite. While the Irish Question remains undecided, though more than a generation has passed by since it commenced; and while the Corn Question has stood over until argument on the subject is exhausted: In the West India Question—where, wrong measures being once taken, all remedy is hopeless—the parties whose whole property is at stake cannot be allowed more than the lapse of a few weeks, to put on record all their objections to the most essential innovations.

This presents an anomaly in the history of public measures, and it can only be accounted for by supposing that ministers, amid their many duties, have completely undervalued the importance of the measure now pending. This conclusion is confirmed by what is understood to be their language to independent members of the legislature whose suffrage they solicit in future discussion. They say the principal opposition of the West Indians is no more than idle and transient clamour. It is merely of a piece with what has been always witnessed. When the abolition of the slave-trade was under discussion, did we not hear the cry, that our ancient colonies would be ruined? That great

measure was carried, yet no ruin ensued. When
the Registry Bill was brought in, had we not a
similar clamour, that the most dangerous excitement among the slaves would be the consequence?
That point, too, was carried; yet no such direful
evils attended it. Again, when the recent Amelioration Clauses were proposed, how furious was
the opposition in the colonies,—the proprietors
there were to be utterly ruined. Many of these
clauses have since been enacted, even where opposition was strongest at the first, and yet no
injury or change has taken place! What is the
inference in regard to compulsory manumission?
We have strenuous opposition at present, it is
true; but when the measure is once carried, that
will soon subside, and all the frightful features of
danger which have alarmed the colonists will turn
out to be mere phantoms of the imagination.

Now, in answer, may we not allege, in the first
place, that the objections urged against those former
measures were not groundless. Our abolition of
the slave-trade, without securing the effectual concurrence of foreign powers in a similar act, has
transferred from British to foreign colonies the
principal supply of Europe with sugar, and without
the smallest benefit to Africa. The Registry Bills
are an enormous tax on our impoverished colonies,
and it is not to them we owe the extinction of our
colonial slave-trade· Of our recent Amelioration

Clauses, the effect in diminishing production is as yet more certain than that of increased benefit to the negro-population.

In the second place, may we not pronounce that the case we are now submitting is very different from any of those cited?

But in this age of superficiality, where all laborious investigation seems exploded, and when a well-turned period of declamation in Parliament sways the nation, let us take another mode of pointing out the difference of this case.

In those important measures which were passed some time back, the Government carried a great number of colonial proprietors living in this country along with them. How different, then, on *primâ facie* evidence, must be the nature and bearings of the measure now proposed, when colonial proprietors, who have always acted with ministers, are constrained, as a solemn duty in defence of their properties and of their families, to oppose it strenuously! It is evident, that to occasion such a feeling, there must be something in the measure alarmingly important, and demanding the most cautious scrutiny.

In former times, the letters sent out by colonial proprietors in England to their friends in the colonies impressed upon the latter, to do all that they were able, to silence clamour in England; but with regard to compulsory manumission, the lesser evil I is chosen, and the admonition is, " Beware of passing this measure, and thus committing yourselves by your own act. *Throw all the responsibility upon ministers, that you may hereafter have full claims for indemnification.*"

The question then resolves itself into this,—Are ministers, considering the situation in which they are placed, and having a due regard to their own fame, prepared to take this responsibility upon themselves? Do they rely upon the passing opinions of the day for their support? Lord Bathurst says, in his despatches, that the colonial legislature " may be assured, that from the final accomplishment of this object this country will not be diverted."

Now it may be true that, with the unthinking populace, the extinction of slavery is desired; but what practical statesman would take this vague expression of feeling for his guide? It may safely be affirmed, that the intelligent portion of the community are aware of the difficulties, and expect from Government, not what is theoretically to be desired, but what is practically and wisely attainable. They are not prepared to lose our West India colonies, which are believed to contribute largely to the prosperity and strength of the kingdom; nor are they at all disposed to inflict injustice upon their fellow-subjects, knowing well, that whatever odium may now attach to the colonial proprietor,

the charge of having countenanced slavery is one
which he shares with the whole British nation.

But it ought further to be known, and well re-
flected on by His Majesty's ministers, that humane
and enlightened individuals, not anxious for the political so much as the moral grandeur of the country,
who waive every notion of expediency, and consider
the cause of humanity as paramount, are beginning
to entertain doubts as to the wisdom of the proceedings of Government.

This is not vague opinion, but is founded on
weighty reasons.

FIRST : That it is the object of British humanity
to exalt the entire African race, and to accomplish
it as a matter of genuine philanthropy in the most
general and efficient manner.

It appears by parliamentary documents, that as
cultivation, during some years past, has decreased
in the British colonies, precisely in the same degree
has the slave-trade of foreigners increased.

To ruin or deteriorate the British colonies is thus
to encourage the horrors of the slave-trade, and to
increase the sum of African suffering.

Therefore, it being the object of the British
nation to abridge that suffering, and not to make a
mere display of sensibility, if the proposed measures can be proved to be destructive of cultivation
in the British colonies, their spirit must be pro-

nounced to be contrary to the sentiments of the country.

And, SECONDLY : That having long since committed the crime of transporting the negroes to our West-India colonies, it is expected by the British nation, that the welfare of future generations will be contemplated ; and that, hereafter, a black society may be witnessed, possessing in itself the attributes, moral, intellectual, and political, of a civilized people.

So strongly does this sentiment pervade the nation, that it is common to hear the inquiry— "What are the negroes to do when free?" implying the belief that rash interference may have proceeded far to accomplish the object, but that judicious legislation has stopped short on the threshold.

If we were to make an appeal to Lord Bathurst, and to all who have taken an active part in the promotion of compulsory manumission, must they not acknowledge, that since the agitation of the subject in 1823, a considerable and perceptible change has taken place in public opinion, in consequence of the inquiry relative to free labour; and that the idea of having a free negro peasantry labouring under a tropical climate for hire is impracticable and hopeless.

Does not, then, the whole question depend on free labour ?

We cannot but infer, that when the relations and consequences of granting freedom to the negroes by compulsion are fully understood in all their widely-spreading effects, the opinion of the country will be as strongly expressed in reprobation, as Earl Bathurst pronounces it at present to be in approbation of the speedy adoption of the measure.

Without any disrespect it may be stated, that some of our ministers, who are upborne by the current of public applause, have had sufficient experience of the fickleness of popularity. Let us recall to mind the wise precept of Mr. Canning in 1819—" Speak not the *will* of the populace, but consult their *benefit.*"

We appeal to each member of parliament to further this counsel. The question of negro *emancipation* is virtually before them. It is conceived, by all those whose properties are at stake, to be presented in its most objectionable form, and they unanimously oppose it. Before deciding on the subject, let every member reflect on the sentiments of two of our greatest statesmen.

Mr. Pitt, in every discussion in which negro-emancipation was agitated, pronounced, that it was an act which must "flow from the master alone."

When that presiding genius of the country's commercial greatness was no more—when Mr. Fox had coalesced with Lord Grenville,—and above all, when the whole anti-colonial party, with Mr. Wilberforce at its head, had joined his ranks, Mr. Fox, in the full tide of his popularity and his power, declared—

" That the idea of an act of parliament to emanci-
" pate the slaves in the West Indies, *without the*
" *consent and concurrent.feeling of all parties con-*
" *cerned,* BOTH IN THIS COUNTRY AND IN THAT, would
" not only be mischievous in its consequences, but
" totally extravagant in its conception, as well as
" impracticable in its execution."

THE END.